THE PEOPLE AND THE
BRITISH ECONOMY
1830–1914

RODERICK FLOUD is an economic historian who has taught at
Cambridge University, Birkbeck College, London, and
Stanford University, California. He pioneered the use of
computers and statistics to study history. His recent work,
Height, Health and History (with K. Wachter and A.
Gregory) uses the changing height of the British popula-
tion since 1750 to describe and analyse changes in living
standards. Since 1988 he has been Provost of London
Guildhall University.

OPUS General Editors

Christopher Butler
Robert Evans
John Skorupski

OPUS books provide concise, original, and authoritative introductions to a wide range of subjects in the humanities and sciences. They are written by experts for the general reader as well as for students.

THE PEOPLE AND THE
BRITISH ECONOMY
1830–1914

Roderick Floud

Oxford   New York
OXFORD UNIVERSITY PRESS
1997

Oxford University Press, Great Clarendon Street, Oxford OX2 6DP

Oxford New York

Athens Auckland Bangkok Bogota Bombay
Buenos Aires Calcutta Cape Town Dar es Salaam
Delhi Florence Hong Kong Istanbul Karachi
Kuala Lumpur Madras Madrid Melbourne
Mexico City Nairobi Paris Singapore
Taipei Tokyo Toronto

and associated companies in
Berlin Ibadan

Oxford is a trade mark of Oxford University Press

British Library Cataloguing in Publication Data

Data available

Library of Congress Cataloging in Publication Data

Floud, Roderick.
The people and the British economy, 1830–1914 / Roderick Floud.
"OPUS"—P. ii.
Includes bibliographical references and index.
1. Income—Great Britain—History. 2. Consumption (Economics)—
Great Britain—History. 3. Great Britain—Population—History.
4. Great Britain—Economic conditions—19th century. 5. Great
Britain—Economic conditions—20th century. I. Title.
HC260.I5F56 1997   339.4'7'0941—dc21   96-52762
ISBN 0-19-289210-X

1 3 5 7 9 10 8 6 4 2

Typeset by Best-set Typesetter Ltd., Hong Kong
Printed in Great Britain
on acid-free paper by
Biddles Ltd
Guildford & King's Lynn

To Eric Hobsbawm

PREFACE

This book is a personal interpretation of the history of the British economy from 1830 to 1914. It relies, therefore, on the research and writing of many hundreds of economists and historians who have explored every aspect of the Victorian and Edwardian period and who, particularly in the last twenty-five years, have revised many aspects of our knowledge of that period. I have been fortunate to work with many of those historians and economists, in particular in producing collectively *The Economic History of Britain since 1700*, edited by myself and Deirdre McCloskey, and I have been greatly influenced by their work. They will, I am sure, recognize many of their insights and ideas in this book and will, I trust, pardon the borrowings which I have made and the simplifications which have been necessary.

I am particularly grateful for the research assistance which I have received from Roy Edwards, and for the friendly and helpful criticism of early drafts by Stanley Engerman, Deian Hopkin, Sarah Palmer, and Barry Supple. Oxford University Press has waited patiently while my colleagues at London Guildhall University have helped me to balance the demands of writing and leading a University. My wife, Cynthia, has criticized, questioned, suggested new lines of approach, and stiffened my resolve; she has, as always, my love and gratitude. My children, Lydia and Sarah, have been supportive as ever. Last, I am honoured that Eric Hobsbawm, colleague, friend and one of the greatest of British historians, has allowed me to dedicate this book to him.

CONTENTS

LIST OF FIGURES

INTRODUCTION

The inspiration for this book comes from a founder of economics and economic history, Adam Smith, who wrote in 1776 that 'Consumption is the sole end of and purpose of all production . . . The maxim is so perfectly self-evident, that it would be absurd to attempt to prove it.'[1] In that spirit, this book concentrates on people rather than on things; it describes the overall income and wealth of Britain, its growth, and how that annual income and accumulated wealth was produced by and distributed between different people in the population. Population growth has a central place, as do the changes in home and workplace which transformed the lives of successive generations in Victorian and Edwardian Britain.

Most economic history, by contrast, is written as the history of production. It describes how land, labour, and capital, the so-called factors of production, are combined to produce the total output of the economy. Output is often narrowly defined, so that there is a concentration on material objects—things—or, even more narrowly, on things which are traded between nations. Services, which are more difficult to measure, or goods which are traded only within the domestic economy, receive less attention. Thus, in *The Workshop of the World* by J. D. Chambers, the excellent small volume of 1961 which this book seeks to bring up to date, pride of place is given to machine industry while retailing, the dairy industry, or the growth of the professions receive little or no mention.

Like all maxims, Adam Smith's is less self-evident than it looks. The changes between 1830 and 1914 in methods of production and in the things which were produced cannot be divorced from the changes in consumption which took place at the same time. They are, indeed, two sides of the same coin; demand and supply interact in the market and in the process of economic change. Moreover, Smith's statement makes sense to modern eyes only if investment—such expenditure on buildings, machines, the services of government and people as will produce benefits at some time to come—is seen as consumption delayed to the future. But, with these qualifications, the maxim still directs our attention to the central purpose of economic life and economic growth: the improvement in the condition of the people.

This book owes another debt to Adam Smith, for it covers the period when Britain was an 'open economy' under the influence of the doctrines of free trade which he advocated in preference to barriers to the free movement of labour, capital, and goods. These tariff and other barriers, most of which had been erected under the influence of mercantilist economic ideas, were largely removed between 1830 and 1860, to be reinstated for the most part only after 1914. During this time, although the connection is by no means clear, Britain became the world's major trading nation, carrier of the majority of the world's goods, by far the largest investor overseas and the centre of the world's financial system. It was an exceptional time in the history of the country and one to which many look back, even a hundred years later, with nostalgia. This book seeks to describe and assess what was achieved in those eighty-five years.

It is, therefore, a book about change. Writing about change can be dangerous, for it can imply that all is for the better, part of an ineluctable progress from past to present. Not all change in the Victorian and Edwardian period was also improvement, as the thousands who choked in the smog of early-twentieth-century cities could attest. It is equally dangerous to dwell on the differences between the Britain of 1914 and that of 1830 and thus to obscure both the myriad of events between those two dates and the complexity of the economy and society at each date. But to write history is to simplify and all that one can hope is that the simplification is as much to the taste and illumination of the reader as Adam Smith's was to the author.

1

INCOME AND WEALTH

Economic growth

In 1914 the economy of the United Kingdom produced nearly seven times as many goods and services as it had done in 1830. During that time the population doubled. As a result, the average amount produced, and then consumed or invested, by a member of the UK population rose by nearly three and a half times. This means that, after taking account of inflation and deflation of prices during the period, the average person—man, woman, or child—was nearly three and a half times better off in 1914 than in 1830. This is the central fact, shown in Figure 1.1, which this book tries to describe and explain.

But first, what does it mean? This question has two parts—how is the calculation done and what impact did this increase have? Calculations of this kind are made by adding up either the total value of prices paid for each of very large numbers of goods and services or, alternatively, adding up the wages and incomes of all the people who made those goods, provided those services, or benefited from owning assets overseas. The two methods should produce the same result, since what is sold is also bought, at the same price. Both methods use information only about what is bought and sold; they do not reflect the value of goods and services which are not normally paid for, such as the housework of women, the vegetables produced in the back garden, and the care of the sick or elderly by family members. Nor do they reflect the range of goods or the benefits of choice, because the calculations add up indiscriminately the value of all kinds of

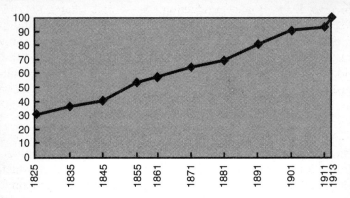

FIG. 1.1   Output/Population in the United Kingdom, 1825–1913

goods and services. They do not necessarily reflect all improvements in the quality of what is produced. Last, they reveal little about whether people had to work harder to secure their larger incomes and consumption. The size of that growth, 3.3 times, is therefore spuriously exact.

But it is also large. Because the average person in the population became so much better off, people were healthier and longer-lived; their lives were spent in better housing, their cities were better provided with roads, public buildings, and transport, they ate more of a greater range of produce, and could spend more of their time in leisure and less at work. The change in all these and other aspects of life was not as rapid as it has been in the twentieth century, since the end of the First World War, but it was very large by the standards of what had gone before.

Part of the change was in the technology of work and everyday life. The year 1825 was the start of the 'railway age'; by 1914 railway tracks reached almost every part of the country and travel by rail was beginning to face competition from the motor car, motor bus, and lorry. Lighting by gas was in its infancy in 1830; by 1914 electric lighting was a feature of many homes while power from electricity and oil was well on the way to replacing the steam and water power which had driven industry in 1830. By 1914 mass production was normal, though not universal, in manufacturing industries and was based on the standardization of parts made by tools whose development had only just begun in 1830; even the screw-thread, that vital part of any domestic appliance, building, or machine, had not been standardized by 1830. There was, in that year, no universal postal system; by 1914 the telegraph was ubiquitous and the telephone no longer a curiosity.

Another part of the change was in the relations of Britain with the wider world. The country's growing income and wealth allowed it to acquire and maintain an overseas empire, 'on which the sun never sets' and to invest in that empire's economic development or, sometimes, deterioration into a state of dependency. In time, this was to threaten some home industries, as when the Indian cotton industry began in the twentieth century to supplant Lancashire, but before 1914 the home country benefited enormously from the wider range of cheaper goods which flowed from India, Africa, Australasia, and Canada. This increased flow of goods was merely a part of the expansion of overseas trade, and of investment in economic development, both within the formal Empire and in what came to be known as the 'informal Empire', areas such as most of Latin America over which the UK had no political control but over whose economies it exercised great influence. Throughout the world British people and British funds built ports, railways, and new cities and established plantations, ranches, and factories.

Economic growth revealed itself in domestic life. In 1830 the cities were expanding rapidly but life in them was near to collapse under the impact of poor building, inadequate transport, badly constructed or non-existent water and sewerage systems, and chaotic patterns of local government. By 1914 housing conditions were greatly improved by the development of the suburbs, linked with town centres and industrial areas by rail, tram, and bus. Houses were less crowded and were more often provided with bathrooms, lavatories, and improved kitchens. Local government was a source of pride and municipal enterprise provided water, power, and light.

In working life, economic growth was reflected in the rise of large enterprises, both in manufacturing and in services such as retailing, transport, and wholesale distribution. It was still very exceptional in 1830 for anyone to work in a factory or workshop employing more than ten people and the staffs of the stately homes of England matched in number the work force of most manufacturers. By 1914, led by the railways, firms with several thousand employees were no longer unusual; their existence had made it necessary for employers to develop new methods of management. However, there had actually been little change in the importance of manufacturing within the overall economy; the main difference in working life between 1830 and 1914 lay in the rapid decline in the agricultural labour force and a balancing increase in the proportion of men and women working in the service industries such as retailing, banking, and transport. This was the great age of personal and domestic service, but it also saw the rise of new professions and of what came to be called the 'shopocracy'.

Above all, economic growth was manifest in the physique of the people. After a check to increase in the average height of the population between 1830 and 1860 as the problems of the cities were tackled, the population grew steadily taller, a sure sign of improved living conditions and more food. In 1830, judging by their stunted and wasted appearance, a significant proportion of the population was severely malnourished; by 1914 that proportion had diminished but not disappeared. By 1914, again, people were healthier during their longer lives; infant death remained a scourge and source of great distress until the end of the nineteenth century, but the infant death rate was declining and the average lifespan of those who had survived infancy was rising rapidly. The impact of both endemic and epidemic diseases was diminishing under the assaults of improvements both in public health and hygiene and in nutrition, although the impact of the medical revolutions of the twentieth century was still to come.

On the other hand, the economy and society of 1914 were still very poor by the standards of the end of the twentieth century; the average annual wage bought nearly five-and-a-half times as much in 1991 as it had done in 1914.[1] Britain was a divided country, in which extremes of wealth and poverty coexisted, often in a state of mutual fear and incomprehension. It was a precarious society, in which the seasons or the mysterious alternation between boom and slump could greatly alter the prospects of employment and with them family incomes and lifestyles, for most of the population had little opportunity to save against a rainy day.

Nor, of course, was the progression from 1830 to 1914 a smooth one. The fortunes of industries, the nature of work and life, changed at different speeds throughout those eighty-five years. The picture therefore needs to be drawn in greater detail.

The pattern of growth

In the nineteenth as in the twentieth century, the economy alternated between boom and slump. So regular did the alternation appear to be, and so much did it seem to be tied to the fortunes of overseas trade, that it came to be known as 'the trade cycle', although in fact it affected much more than exports and imports.

Every nine years, approximately, the economy moved through a cycle from depression to recovery and back to depression. Although the total output of the economy and, therefore, the total incomes of the population were greater at the end of each cycle, the intervening period was one of great distress for some people and a cause of concern for many others. In the downward part of the cycle, industry and agriculture found it more difficult to sell goods, or could do so only by reducing prices and cutting their expenses; in an age when most costs were those of labour, this meant unemployment for some, short-time working and uncertainty for others.

Each of the eleven major business cycles between 1815 and 1914 had its own characteristics and its own victims. In the 1830s there was great distress in manufacturing districts; in the 1860s the hardest hit were in the financial sector and, for different reasons, in cotton manufacture; in the 1880s agriculture suffered and in the 1890s manufacturing. But a state of crisis in another

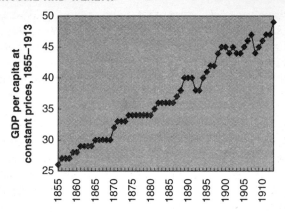

FIG. 1.2   Output (Gross Domestic Product) per capita at constant prices, 1855–1913

sector, or the memory of it in one's own, coloured the lives of every Victorian employer and employee.

The short-term cycles were particularly, though not exclusively, related to the performance of British exports. Underlying them, however, were deeper and longer-term influences on the state of the economy, which intertwined with and sometimes exacerbated the effect of the cycles on discrete groups of the population and helped to produce longer cycles in the economy. One of the most notable features of the late nineteenth century, for example, was the decline in the prices of many goods between 1873 and 1896, which helped to give that period the name the 'Great Depression', although its consequences were much less severe than those of the Great Depression which affected the whole world in the 1930s. While prices had fluctuated to some extent from year to year between 1830 and 1873, there was no clear trend, but between 1873 and 1896 prices fell by 20 per cent, before rising again by nearly 18 per cent between 1896 and 1914. Such changes—overall in a downward direction—pale into insignificance compared to the sharp upward movements within the inflationary periods of the twentieth century, but they must have seemed dramatic at the time. If opinions differ on the precise causes, it appears that a shortage of gold was a major factor. At the time many of the leading countries were 'on the gold standard', in other words, their paper currencies had to be backed by a quantity of gold held in the central banks. On top of other monetary changes, the prices of individual commodities were affected by the development of new technologies and new sources of supply.[2]

The most notable long-term adjustment, for example, affected workers in agriculture, still the largest single occupation in the 1830s. Before then, farmers and landlords had benefited from the effects of a rising population earning larger incomes, which increased demands for food. This was reinforced by tariffs on imported foodstuffs, which at times were so high that they almost amounted to the prohibition of imports. Farmers responded to rising demand by a variety of measures which together have come to be known as the 'Agricultural Revolution': they completed the enclosure of the open fields of the Middle Ages, improved stock breeding methods, developed new crops, and adapted their cropping to the soil types of the different regions.

After the 1830s investment in agriculture continued but there was increasing public dissatisfaction with the tariff protection enjoyed by wheat producers through the operation of the Corn Laws. Their repeal in 1846 by the Prime Minister, Sir Robert Peel, who split the Conservative Party on the issue, was at least symbolically the centrepiece of the movement towards free trade. By the 1860s, the repeal of the Corn Laws and of other tariffs had combined with the development of many new sources of imported food in Eastern Europe, the Americas, Australasia, and the Tropics and were beginning to erode the markets of home producers. The new technology of refrigeration reinforced this trend. Initially, British agriculture wilted under the pressure, but farmers gradually came to realize the need to adapt, to concentrate on producing milk, other dairy products and vegetables which did not face foreign competition, or to emphasize the high quality of Scotch beef compared with Argentinian imports.

Agricultural prices fell between 1873 and 1896 by over 40 per cent, much faster than other prices in the economy. In an effort to cut costs, farmers and landlords focused on their major cost, that of employing labour. They chose new products which required fewer workers and mechanized tasks such as the harvesting and threshing of corn. As a result, the number of workers employed in agriculture fell sharply in the last thirty years of the nineteenth century, and the incomes of farm workers lagged behind those of other groups in the population. Even so, many landlords and farmers could not fully compensate for falling prices and suffered falling incomes or, at the extreme, were forced into bankruptcy.

Agricultural change was, however, only the most obvious of many structural changes which affected the population. Landlords and farmers had vocal champions in Parliament, who could describe their plight and call for government assistance, although these pleas fell largely on the deaf ears of government ministers wedded to the principles of free trade. Other groups received less attention, but suffered as much. Just as the years before 1830 had seen the increased use of machines in the spinning and weaving sections of the textile industries, with the reduction to poverty of handloom weavers who had first been made prosperous in the later eighteenth century, so later years saw the introduction of machinery into a wide variety of trades, from hosiery manufacture to mechanical engineering. Depending on the circumstances of the particular trade, this led to the devaluation of previously valued skills or even to the disappearance of whole industries. Changing fashion, in such matters as hats or mourning clothes, could also devastate once prosperous trades.

As industries and occupations declined or disappeared, however, others rose. Although there was a great deal of unemployment between 1830 and 1914, with an impact that was particularly harsh in the depths of each cycle, there is no sign that there was a long-term overall increase in the numbers of the unemployed as a proportion of the working population. That does not rule out patches of increasing misery. There was a great deal of underemployment, in which workers were employed for only part of the week, day, or year; dock-labour in London, Liverpool, and other ports was the most prominent of these casual trades. London in particular became a centre of the 'sweated' trades, in which a 'cheap, overfilled, unskilled labour pool of women and immigrants', working at subsistence wages, fulfilled a mass demand for cheap, ready-made goods.[3] Even in the countryside, employment opportunities for women diminished as men, often working new machines, became dominant in arable cultivation.

In many old industries the number of workers increased while at the same time new industries and occupations emerged. Overall, there were 18.3 million people in the labour force in 1911, compared with 6.9 million in 1841. The unemployed were counted as part of the occupied population, but some married women such as farmers' wives were not, so that these figures probably underestimate the numbers actually at work. A further indication of the increasing scale and complexity of economic life comes from the census, taken regularly every ten years after 1831. While in 1851 the census analysts were instructed to register occupations under 90 headings, by 1911 this had increased to 470, though some new categories were subdivisions of the old. Among the new occupations were four under the heading of electrical workers and several for employment on trams and omnibuses. Each required new skills, each new forms of training, and each had to be slotted into the complex hierarchies of working and social life.

The distribution of income and wealth

Victorian and Edwardian Britain was an unequal society; there were extremes of income and even more of wealth which set members of society apart from, and sometimes against, each other. But inequality in income and wealth was not the only form of inequality. Different geographical regions differed one from the other, while the experience of the old differed greatly from that of the young, and that of the middle-aged from both, while perhaps the greatest differences were between the lives of men and women.

Oddly, in a country which was ruled by a queen, most women were excluded, as they were throughout the world, from the exercise either of political or of economic power. 'Votes for Women' were advocated by members of the Chartist movement of the 1840s, as part of a general programme of political reform. But, although women who owned property could vote in local government elections from 1869, female votes in parliamentary elections did not become practical politics until the Suffragette Movement of the Edwardian period forced the issue on the attention of the public and the First World War altered attitudes. Only in 1928 was female suffrage at the same age as men—then 21—completely achieved. In economic terms, wives and daughters were entirely subservient legally to husbands and fathers at least until the Married Women's Property Acts of the 1870s and 1880s; before then, a woman's economic assets, perhaps from an inheritance, became the property of the husband on marriage, although for the upper classes legal devices such as settlements on marriage gave some protection. Protecting her body took longer; only in 1891 did it become illegal for a man to beat or imprison his wife. Marriage also signalled, for many women, the end of any independent working life, although there were wide variations in practice both within and between different areas and occupations.

Changes in the law do not tell the whole story. In a wide range of occupations, women played a vital role in the labour force, whether or not they received their own wage. In many, such as shopkeeping and farming, they played a full part in directing the enterprise, as they did in many craft occupations where wives still worked with husbands. In factory manufacturing and services, on the other hand, while women's work was both important and increasingly diversified as the century wore on, it became largely distinguished from men's work and, where any semblance of comparison remained, women were much worse paid and segregated in particular jobs. Within the household, too, there were marked divisions of labour. These became even greater when increased incomes gave more leisure and ways of using it which were related to gender.

If gender inequality was fundamental to Victorian and Edwardian society, no less fundamental (though no less variable in detail over the period) was inequality between social and economic classes. The familiar Victorian hymn 'All things bright and beautiful' expressed reality well:

> The rich man in his castle, the poor man at his gate,
> God made them high and lowly and ordered their estate.

Concepts of class were first formulated by theoreticians at the beginning of the nineteenth century; by its end, they permeated the thinking of the whole society. This came about partly through the theories of class enunciated by Karl Marx and other social analysts and partly through the establishment of patterns of behaviour. These served explicitly and sometimes deliberately to set one group of people apart from another. Marx himself was an acute observer of the British society into which he migrated in 1849 and his characterization of social classes based on their relation to the means of production has not been bettered. It has, however, been elaborated by many contemporary observers and historians, through whose studies we can better appreciate the complexities of class and class behaviour and the importance which the emulation of the behaviour of other classes played in the evolution of Victorian society.

Other inequalities were superimposed upon gender and class. British society was not homogeneous and economic opportunities and responses varied greatly from one part of the country to another. The capital city provides one example. Throughout the period, London was one of the foremost manufacturing centres of the country, but some of its most prominent industries in 1830, such as shipbuilding, disappeared completely during this period, supplanted by the new shipyards of Glasgow, Liverpool, and Newcastle. By contrast, the London suburbs and, at the end of the century, new towns such as Welwyn Garden City provided new forms of living based to a large extent on the service industries. In the rest of the country, new manufacturing towns, such as Middlesbrough and Saltaire, were established or grew from insignificant villages. A whole new type of town, the seaside resort, was developed to cater for a wealthier population with more opportunities for leisure. Last, the face of the countryside changed as farming adapted to new demands by developing new crops and new forms of agriculture and horticulture.

Many of these environmental changes perpetuated old inequalities or produced new ones. Early in the period, for example, the lack of planning for what is now called 'infrastructure' helped create the problems of the inner city on a scale hitherto unknown. Early attempts at town and transport planning, such as the building of the railway termini in London or the development of the commercial centre of Birmingham, often made matters worse. The slums were demolished but housing which the working classes could afford was not built in their place. Terrible slums, often within a few hundred metres of the homes, shops and offices of the middle- and upper-classes, persisted well into the twentieth century. They were not hidden, particularly because they were so well depicted by such writers as Charles Dickens, Jack London, and Arthur Morrison, whose *Child of the Jago*, a story of London's East End, is still almost unbearable to read. The denizens of the slums of London and other cities appeared as another race to upper-class observers; they were so stunted and wizened by illness and poverty as to persuade many writers that urban life had bred men and women with a genetic predisposition to degeneracy. Such was the difference in average height that it was literally true that the upper classes looked down on the working classes.

The working classes as a whole lived close to the margin throughout their lives but their patterns of work meant that there were significant inequalities in another form, between different age groups. Living standards in childhood were, of course, dependent upon the income of parents, although child labour was very often a significant part of the family income. This remained true, even though in the 1830s and 1840s the hours of child labour were limited and children were banned from labour in mines and chimneys. The next stage of life, adolescence and before marriage, was probably that of greatest independence and highest disposable income. Marriage and children took their toll and left little spare income until the children themselves began to earn and to leave home but, by that time, the earnings of the main breadwinner might begin to fall under the impact of years of hard physical labour. There was no formal age of retirement and, before the introduction of state old-age pensions in 1908, work continued at a slower pace and for a lesser wage until it became impossible. Then whatever meagre savings had been accumulated would need to be supplemented by help from children; in its absence, men and women would be forced to fall back on the Poor Law, symbolized by the dreaded Workhouse. Poor relief became more punitive after 1834 and throughout the century its administrators continued to try to deter the poor from relying upon it.

There is little sign that the United Kingdom became, between 1830 and 1914, a more equal society, although there is no single way to sum up all the different forms of inequality. While the population became on average 3.3 times richer, the range of incomes around that average did not significantly diminish; the rich remained much richer than the average, the poor much poorer. At the bottom of the range, poverty remained very obvious; up to a third of the population in 1914 had incomes which did not provide them with sufficient food to sustain health throughout the year. At the other extreme, Edwardian society became a byword for what the American economist Thorstein Veblen was later to describe as 'conspicuous consumption',[4] based on high incomes and high levels of inherited wealth. The number of men and women who bequeathed, when they died, estates worth more than £1 million rose from thirty-three in 1883–1893 to sixty-eight in 1900–1910, although these figures understate the true level of wealth in society because of undervaluations of land and because gifts made to relatives before death are omitted. These 'super-rich' were the tip of that 17 per cent of men and women who died in 1900–1 and left enough property for their wills to be subject to probate. The security which wealth gave to such people contrasted with the almost complete insecurity of the life of the poor. Growth in the economy was certainly a fact, but to many it must have been difficult to perceive.

The sources of growth

Why did the British economy grow as it did? The answer to this question is both obvious and elusive. The obvious answer is that a larger population implies both more workers to produce and more consumers to consume. The prospect of a larger market stemming from population growth encourages businessmen, landowners, and financiers to invest in new factories, machinery, and transport facilities. This allows more food and manufactured goods to be produced, and the wages paid to those who make or grow these products then allow them to be bought and consumed. Some of the products can also be sold overseas, in exchange for other products to be consumed here.

At the same time, the fact that on average every person in Britain was richer in 1914 than in 1830 implies that economic growth did much more than run parallel with an increasing population. Each worker in 1914 produced much more than each worker in 1830; each consumer in 1914 consumed much more than each consumer in 1830. This is where the answer becomes elusive, because there are several logical possibilities which could explain why this should have occurred. At one extreme, the growth could have occurred because each worker continued to work in the same way but simply worked harder or, perhaps, for more hours in the day or more days in the year. At the other extreme, each worker might have been provided with equipment or machinery to change the way in which he or she worked and to allow more to be produced; if the new equipment or machinery cost less than the value of the additional products, then there was a benefit to the economy.

In practice the economy grew because of a combination of these factors and of changes in between the two extremes. Workers worked harder, in part because they were better fed and better educated; at the same time, they were provided with increasing amounts of complex equipment which enabled them to produce more for a given amount of effort. This equipment cost money to invent, manufacture, and implement, but made it possible for workers to produce goods which were worth more than the cost of the equipment itself. In other words, the economy became more efficient. It was better in 1914 at combining natural resources, workers, and capital to produce output than it had been in 1830.

This is a very abstract statement. It is possible, for at least part of the period, to be somewhat more precise. Between 1856 and 1873, surprisingly, the total amount of hours worked in the British economy did not increase, because an increase of 0.8 per cent on average each year in the numbers of workers was exactly balanced by a reduction in the number of hours that they worked in each year and by a slight increase in unemployment. However, the productive capacity of workers improved by 1.4 per cent on average each year, principally because as a whole the workers were older and more experienced, because they were better educated, and because they worked more intensively during their shorter hours. As a result of investment, the buildings, equipment, and machinery which those workers used increased by 1.9 per cent each year. Putting these two—workers and equipment—together, the total input into the economy increased by 1.6 per cent each year, but the total output increased by 2.2 per cent each year. The gap between change in inputs and in outputs, 2.2 per cent minus 1.6 per cent = 0.6 per cent per annum, measures the increasing efficiency of the economy.

In the following period, 1873–1913, the situation changed. Man- and woman-hours increased by 0.9 per cent on average each year, exactly the same figure as the increase in workers and, in addition, the productive capacity of workers improved by 0.8 per cent per annum. The total increase in the labour input was therefore 1.7 per cent on average each year. Buildings, machinery, and equipment increased by 1.9 per cent each year. Putting the two together gives a total increase in inputs to the economy of 1.8 per cent each year, but the total output increased by the same proportion so that there was, by this calculation, no increase overall in the efficiency of the economy.[5] The period 1873–1913 was therefore an unusual one, unique in peacetime between 1856 and 1973 in experiencing no increase overall in efficiency.

Even these calculations are, however, in some sense abstractions, the result of a myriad individual actions in workshops, factories, farms, and offices. Inevitably, transformations in working practices greatly improved efficiency in some jobs such as those in engineering; some saw the invention of entirely new products such as bicycles; some such as coal mining, conversely, experienced such difficulties that they became less efficient. The calculations do, however, point to the importance of two continuing changes, the improvement in the quality of labour and the increase in capital investment. These will be discussed again later in this book.

The performance of the economy

Despite the apparent success of Britain as the country of the first Industrial Revolution, economic historians have devoted thousands of pages in books and learned journals to an apparently simple question: 'Should economic growth have been faster?'

There has been little dissent, either at the time or since, from the view that the economy performed well until the 1860s or 1870s. There were checks to growth and bad periods such as the 'hungry forties', but overall the upward trend was clear, as was the superiority of British industry to that of other nations. But increasingly gloomy discussion and analysis of the performance of the economy began as early as the 1860s. The Great Exhibition held in London in 1851 celebrated the technical achievements of the world, with exhibits from many countries, but the overwhelming impression which it created, and was indeed designed to create, was of the superior strength of the British economy and the technological lead which it held over all other countries. However, as international exhibitions succeeded one another in the following decades, doubts began to grow. As early as the Paris Exhibition of 1867, British observers were worried by the technological achievements of the United States and, later, their fears centred on machinery and industrial processes devised in Germany.

Concerns about rising foreign competition were widely expressed in the last decades of the nineteenth century, although the statistics which now demonstrate the strength of that competition were not compiled until after the Second World War. What contemporary writers were able to see, therefore, was the invention in France, Germany, and the United States of new methods of production and new products with the potential to supplant British goods in export markets or which were imported for use in British industry. The burgeoning engineering industry was a particular source of concern; in 1851 there were essentially no rivals to Britain in the working of metals, but by the 1880s and 1890s even if Britain retained its hold on textile equipment, America and Germany were strong competitors in machine tools, arms manufacture, and transport equipment. The German chemical industry came to hold a dominant position in the production of dyestuffs and America established a lead in some, though not all, branches of the new electrical industries.

It is now clear that the British economy was continuing to grow, though at a lesser rate than the economies of other countries which were able to imitate and build on Britain's earlier achievements. In many ways, this was to the benefit of the British economy, which was able to expand the range of goods which it could import for the benefit of the population, to learn from technological achievements and new processes pioneered in other countries, and to export its goods to the populations of other countries which were themselves becoming richer. These were, as many politicians and economists emphasized at the time, the benefits of free trade. But, particularly at times of economic depression, these benefits were apparently insufficient to offset the damage which one or other foreign industry seemed to be doing in markets which had hitherto been served by Britain. Landlords and farmers were especially vociferous in the 1880s and 1890s, although with little success as the British population remained wedded to cheap food.

But fear of foreign competition or even of foreign domination was pervasive and affected many areas of political and economic life. In education, for example, successive enquiries called attention to deficiencies in the British system which were only partly remedied by the introduction of universal primary education in the 1870s. The Civil Service and the Army were reformed partly in response to what was thought to be German efficiency. At the end of the century, there was a public outcry when the poor health of the soldiers recruited for the South African War was revealed. Unless this was remedied, it was argued, Britain's economy and national power would be eroded and there would be danger of economic decline or even foreign invasion.

The figures quoted in the last section show that there was a failure, between 1873 and 1913, to increase the efficiency of the economy. But detailed study of a number of British industries has not uncovered many examples of the failure of British entrepreneurs to exploit opportunities for new products or new processes and thus to make themselves and the country richer than it was. There certainly were differences in the way in which, for example, British and American factories produced cotton goods, but many of the differences can be explained by the type of cloth which was being produced or by different costs of labour and machinery. Similarly, studies of British investment behaviour have not convicted British financiers of the charge, often levelled against them, that they neglected domestic industry in favour of sending their funds to build foreign ports or railways. Even British agriculture, long considered to be stuck in the mud, was able to compete effectively with foreign producers once it had completed its process of changing specialization.

If such detailed studies have failed to demonstrate that British industrialists and businessmen could have done much better, there still remain nagging doubts that there were more systematic failures of British society which, if remedied, could have made the country richer than it was. The class structure, the educational system, the trade unions, systems of management, the railways have all been studied in the search for culprits but the answers have not been convincing. More fancifully, it has been argued that the British preferred leisure to hard work, that they hankered after a rural idyll rather than the rewards of industrial capitalism, or that they were so much in thrall to a landowning aristocracy that they aspired only to own land and thus to distance themselves from the world of manufacturing. It is impossible to argue, of course, that the British economy could not have grown faster. It grew faster in the period between 1830 and 1914 than it had done during the period of the Industrial Revolution which preceded it, but more slowly than it was to do for most of the twentieth century. It also grew more slowly than the economies of most other industrializing countries. But the gap was not so great that it left the British population markedly poorer than it might have been, nor so obvious that a single cause or even a multiplicity of causes can easily be identified.

2

UNCERTAINTY AND RISK

The experience of change

With hindsight, the growth of the economy between 1830 and 1914 appears to have been continuous and even reasonably smooth. Those men and women who lived and worked in that period experienced it as one of change, risk, and uncertainty. It is a common human trait to describe, and perhaps to deplore, one's own age as a period of unprecedented change and to look back to a previous 'golden age' of stability and certainty. But those who lived in the middle of the nineteenth century were right to see their age as one of pervasive change, from which no sector of the economy or of society was immune. The great philosopher and economist John Stuart Mill wrote in 1831 that his was 'an age of transition', a fact which was 'obvious a few years ago only to the more discerning: at present it forces itself upon the most unobservant.' He saw change itself as 'the first of the leading peculiarities of the present age.'[1]

The Victorians retained an ambivalent attitude to change; they celebrated it because it brought increasing control over the forces of nature and they deplored the way in which it upset established patterns of social relationships. Change bred insecurity and exacerbated the uncertainties of what was in any case, for the majority, an insecure and risky life. Risk can, of course, be enlivening; successful risk-taking lay at the heart of the success of the many businessmen who were celebrated in the books of Samuel Smiles. They were able to triumph over, or at least to cope with, the vicissitudes of the economy and their success must not be forgotten. Much of the rest of this book is, in a sense, their story.

Household and family

For the majority of the population, however, life was lived close to the margin. The extent of economic growth between 1830 and 1914 should not obscure the fact that, certainly at the beginning and even at the end of the period, much more than half of the population lived at or close to levels at which their health was affected by lack of food, warmth, or housing.

In the early years of the twentieth century, J. Seebohm Rowntree conducted a study of poverty in York which has become a classic of social investigation. Rowntree attempted to establish a definition of poverty which was based not on relative criteria of wealth or poverty but on the absolute criterion of the ability to live, grow, and work. He argued that families living in poverty could be divided into two groups. First, 13 per cent of the population were 'families whose total earnings are insufficient to obtain the minimum necessaries for the maintenance of merely physical efficiency.' Second, about another 14 per cent were 'families whose total earnings would be sufficient for the maintenance of merely physical efficiency were it not that some portion of it is absorbed by other expenditure, either useful or wasteful.'[2]

Taking the two groups together, a total of 27 per cent of the population lived in such a state that they could not work a normal day, because they were so malnourished, while their children could not be fed enough to grow at a normal rate. Charles Booth's survey of London[3] at the same time confirmed that about 30 per cent of the population was living in this way. These families were actually living below the margin.

Similar studies had not been conducted early in the nineteenth century, but there is every reason to believe that conditions were worse, and that an even larger proportion of the population then lived for some parts of the year below subsistence level. Recent research into the growth of children suggests that working-class children were severely stunted and that they achieved average heights in adolescence which are now surpassed by over 97 per cent of modern children. Nineteenth-century diets confirm the paucity of protein and energy, while the level of endemic and epidemic disease attests to the low resistance of the population to infection.

The course of population change is considered in detail in the next chapter. For the moment, what is of importance is that, while 30 per cent lived below the margin, perhaps a further 40 per cent or even more lived so close to the margin that they could be, and often were, forced below it by a variety of life events. Within the context of household and family, the most solemn occasion was the death, disablement, or illness of any breadwinner but particularly of the main earner, usually but by no means invariably the husband and father. Such an event was a very real possibility, certainly as real a cause of the break-up of the family unit as divorce is now at the end of the twentieth century.

It has been estimated, for example, that at least 11 per cent of all children born in 1831 had lost either their father or mother by death before the age of 10, and that 17 per cent had done so by the age of 15.[4] The life recorded on a tombstone:

> Sixteen years a Maiden
> One twelve months a Wife
> One half hour a Mother
> Then I lost my Life

was not unusual in an age when maternal mortality was so frequent a cause of death. The death of father or mother, intensely distressing in itself, might well also lead to poverty and to the break-up of the family unit. The fear of death, and of the catastrophe which it might bring, must have been ever-present in the Victorian household. In 1850, for example, 80 men and women of working age died for every 1,000 living, a rate of 1 in 12.5, while 75 of every 1,000 infants and children died, a rate of 1 in 13.3. In 1980, by contrast, only 1 in 44 of those of working age died, and only 1 in 281 infants and children.[5] In 1850, any adult had to reckon with the possibility that they, their husband, wife, or child, might not survive to the next year.

The extent of disablement and serious illness is more difficult to gauge, but the evidence of friendly and benefit societies, whose members and subscribers tended to come from the more prosperous sections of the working and lower middle classes, is that there was a serious risk of illness severe enough to threaten the household income. It did not, however, even require disease or death to plunge a family into poverty. For many unskilled workers, the mere act of having children or of growing old could have the same effect. As one observer of Huddersfield's woollen handloom weavers put it in 1849: 'if they have young families . . . , that is, families over young to help them by working in the mills, they don't get half enough to eat.'[6] As a result, children were particularly prone to live in poverty; even in 1915, investigators found that while 23.3 per cent of families in Reading lived in Rowntree's first group of those in poverty, that group contained 45 per cent of children under 5.

Families with children were also particularly likely to suffer bad housing conditions and to be poorly clothed. In such circumstances, it was essential to protect the health of the breadwinner, even at the expense of the rest of the family. As Rowntree put it:

We *see* that many a labourer, who has a wife and three or four children, is healthy and a good worker, although he only earns a pound a week. What we do not *see* is that in order to give him enough food, mother and children habitually go short, for the mother knows that all depends upon the wages of her husband.[7]

Even if a family was lucky enough not to suffer illness or death, few could avoid periods of unemployment. Cyclical fluctuations in the economy, seasonal fluctuations in demand, or changes in fashion could all throw men and women out of work. The fact that all working-class families lived close to the margins of subsistence accounts for many aspects of economic and social life. The price of food and other necessities was crucial. Wage-rates did not vary greatly, provided the wage-earner remained employed, but actual earnings and the price of food varied substantially during the year and over the course of economic cycles. With the gradual decline in the employment of women and children in the course of the century, it became more difficult for them to supplement male incomes.

In such circumstances, stratagems to make do became of crucial importance. Expenditure, for many besides Mr Micawber in Dickens's *David Copperfield*, had to be adapted minutely to income. As Leonore Davidoff puts it:

Women's main housekeeping task ... [was] budgeting the precarious income, making it stretch by casual washing, taking in lodgers, piecework, gleaning or whatever came to hand. ... In this situation, a family's standing for credit, for services rendered, loans given and general financial and personal viability, became a critical resource. Women were at the centre of these credit networks whether obtaining tick from shopkeepers or giving and receiving services.[8]

In 1867 a judge in Macclesfield, commenting on the pattern of actions for default on debts, described how: 'A system of credit is absolutely necessary in the manufacturing districts. Seasons of distress recur periodically in these localities, where, but for the facilities provided by the shopkeepers, whole families must starve or become inmates of the workhouse.' Shopkeepers, and their customers, had a joint interest in seeing that the debts were paid, but despite this, in nearly 4 per cent of cases the shopkeeper went to court to secure payment.[9]

Relatively fixed items of spending, such as rent for housing, had to be minimized, a fact which helps to account for the extensive subdivision of houses in Victorian cities and for the prevalence of lodgers; families adjusted the number of rooms which they rented to their current incomes. Rooms and houses were normally rented in England on weekly tenancies, although in Scotland a year was more common, and the life of a working-class family could be one of an endless succession of moves.

Debt was an ever-present reality; it was often necessary to rely on the pawnbroker, where there was anything to pawn, to tide the family over each week. As Asa Briggs observes in his fascinating study of 'Victorian Things', the increase in the number of artefacts meant that there were many more possessions to pawn.[10] The pawnbroker was one aspect of a complex web of working-class institutions designed to help low-income house-holds 'finely balanced on a knife edge of sufficiency' to save in the good times and to borrow in the bad.[11] Despite the urgings of middle-class observers that the working classes should save against the risks of unemployment and old age, many were able to do little more than put aside tiny sums to provide for funeral expenses. Some could not even do this and observers described the consequences: bodies remained unburied for weeks, in homes where normal life had to be carried on around the putre-fying corpse.[12] Even where insurance existed, most policies were for very small sums and did not provide for the costs of illness or old age.

For a few, crime was one response. Despite the view of an influential body of social commentators in the nineteenth cen-tury that crime was the result of original sin or, possibly, of the existence of a so-called criminal class, it is clear that property crime 'increased in times of depression and diminished in times of prosperity: more people stole in hard times than in good.'[13] This was almost certainly also true of prostitution, which disfig-ured many Victorian cities. The upswings and downswings of the trade or business cycles brought with them reductions and then increases in property crime, principally theft; but, in the long-term, the growing prosperity of the second half of the nineteenth century saw a continuing reduction in crime rates. Rates never rose much higher than 450 crimes in a year per 100,000 of the population and declined, by the end of the century, to around 300. Some of this reduction can be attributed to more, and more efficient, policemen, but the fluctuations suggest that improving economic conditions were the primary cause. This interpretation of what are, certainly, ambiguous statistics is confirmed by the fact that crimes of violence and drunkenness show an entirely different pattern. Such crimes were much less common than those against property; they made up only about one-tenth of recorded crime but increased in times of prosperity, decreased in times of depression.

However, even if crime was rare and property crime diminish-ing during the second half of the nineteenth century, fear of crime was certainly widespread, fed by a constant diet of lurid court reports in Victorian newspapers. Although the fears were mostly expressed by the middle classes, it was as always the working classes who were the main victims and therefore the main beneficiaries of the decline in crimes against property. The great Victorian reformer and social observer Edwin Chadwick believed that by the end of the century working-class families could own personal property which, possessed before mid-century, would have 'endangered their lives.'[14] It is no surprise that locks and their improvement were a feature of many of the great exhibitions of Victorian Britain.

Crime was always, however, a very unusual reaction to poverty. Those without were much more likely to resort to public or private charity. In previous ages, the Poor Law had provided a minimal safety net against the consequences of poverty, illness, and old age. From the end of the eighteenth century, indeed, many of the local Poor Law authorities had provided what was known as 'outdoor relief', essentially a supplement to the income of the poorest families, paid to them while they continued to live in their own homes. Alarm on the part of local taxpayers at the cost of this provision, together with an increasing emphasis on economic individualism and the need for those individuals to stand on their own feet rather than to rely on society as a whole, led to the passage in 1834 of the New Poor Law. Although several decades passed before the law took full effect and outdoor relief was never fully abolished, the legislation gradually confined support from the Poor Law to those who were prepared, or rather forced by circumstances, to enter the workhouse. The able-bodied were generally deterred by the workhouse regime, so that by the end of the century workhouses catered almost entirely for the sick, the orphaned, and the old. Charities adopted similar principles so that, by the end of the century, the safety nets provided by society were at a very low level. Charity and the Poor Law were not, therefore, a solution to the risks of life, but a major part of those risks. It was only with the Liberal welfare reforms introduced after 1906 that minimal provision for pensions and unemployment benefit for a small fraction of the workforce began to provide some small security.

Poverty put a family at particular risk. But the household could be a source of danger even for the better-off. Contaminated food was widespread in Victorian Britain and, although it was worst in the local shops used by the poor, the middle classes were not immune from its effects. It was said of one typhoid epidemic that 'the persons who suffered were not of the class among whom fevers are most commonly observed, but were persons in very comfortable positions in society, attended by private medical men, and residing in some of the best houses in the parish.'[15] The cause was probably infected milk, of which the middle classes drank more than the working classes. Milk was widely diluted with water, itself often contaminated, and then coloured with chemicals; its poor quality contributed to the high incidence of infantile diarrhoea and tuberculosis. Towards the end of the nineteenth century, in addition, the desire for pure food led to a search for preservatives, particularly as milk came to be supplied over longer distances by rail. Boracic acid and formalin were great favourites of dairymen, a 40 per cent solution of formaldehyde being added at five ounces to a gallon of milk, the smell and taste being masked by sodium or potassium nitrate; even this did not kill bacteria, but merely slowed the souring of the milk. Despite some public concern, these additives and colourings, toxic in themselves, were not banned until 1912.[16]

But not only food could damage health in the household. As many paintings of the time attest, green was a favourite colour. But green was most easily produced by the liberal application of arsenic, usually in the form of Scheele's Green, of which 700 tons were made in England in 1860 and used in products as diverse as paint, clothes, soap, stuffed animals, lampshades, handkerchiefs, and wallpaper. It was even used to colour confectionery and blancmanges. 'Killer wallpaper' was a particular hazard; in 1871 the *British Medical Journal* claimed that it could be found 'from the palace down to the navvy's hut. It is rare to meet a house where arsenic is not visible on the walls of at least some of the rooms.'[17] Controversy about the resultant dangers raged between the 1850s and 1870s; numerous illnesses and even deaths were attributed to this form of environmental pollution, but calls for legislation to ban the use of arsenic were resisted although, as consumer resistance increased and fashions changed, its use gradually declined.

Outside the home, environmental pollution became an increasingly serious problem, as the growth of the cities and the increasing use of coal in homes and factories created the smog through which Sherlock Holmes and Dr Watson groped their way. In many cities, visible smoke pollution was permanent by the end of the century, while in London, there was no moment in the whole Edwardian period in which it was possible to see the Palace of Westminster along the Thames from Waterloo Bridge, a distance of less than a mile. Respiratory diseases, exacerbated by pollution, were among the major causes of illness and death, while the high incidence of rickets among children of all classes in the inner areas of Victorian cities is a probable indication of their lack of exposure to sunlight.[18] The weakness which was thus caused also contributed to deaths, in particular from whooping-cough.

Work and workplace

If it was within the home and family that many of the risks of Victorian and Edwardian society were most keenly felt, it was in the workplace that many of them had their origins. This was true in the most extreme sense that the chances of death varied greatly between occupations. This had always been true; occupations like mining and fishing were particularly dangerous, as was that classic of child labour, chimney-sweeping. Some of the worst dangers were removed by the effects of legislation in the 1830s and 1840s, but even in the 1860s and 1870s, when approximate statistics become available, occupational differentials in death rates were still very large and the dangers of some occupations very great.

It was safest, in Victorian and Edwardian England, to be a clergyman. In the 1860s, only 6 of every 1,000 clergy died between the ages of 25 and 44. By contrast, 17.5 chimney sweeps, 16.3 file makers, 15 bargemen and watermen, and 12.6 potters died per 1,000 in those occupations. What is more remarkable, and a signal of the failure of society to cope with the old and new risks of working life, is that although each individual occupation became slightly safer, the differentials between them and the safe clergy became greater. By 1900, only 3.4 in every 1,000 clergy aged 25–44 died, but 12 chimney sweeps, 13.4 file makers, 11 bargemen and watermen, and 9 potters (per 1,000 in those occupations). It was then most dangerous to be an innkeeper or inn-servant, 17.9 per 1,000 of whom died, many from the effects of excess alcohol consumption and tuberculosis.

Not all early death stemmed, of course, from the direct effects of working conditions, since low wages also played a part. Nevertheless, decades after the risks of some occupations were described by the Registrar General of Births, Marriages and Deaths, men and women continued to die from the effects of metal poisoning, grit and dust, accidents, and poor ventilation.[19] Match girls died from 'phossy-jaw' as the phosphorus which they put on match heads ate into their faces through their teeth; short of death, the children who were employed for up to fifteen hours a day in the Staffordshire potteries fell prey to lead poisoning, while miners and seamstresses suffered disabling eye defects; needle grinders suffered from 'grinder's asthma' as the stone- and steel-dust entered their lungs.[20] Alcohol, taken to dull the pain of life, could cause danger to others; a drunken winder at the Withy Mills Pit once 'overwound' nine men into the pulleys which drew up the cage in the pitshaft. Even such apparently innocuous occupations as house painting carried hidden dangers, those of poisoning from lead paint described so vividly in Robert Tressell's classic novel of Edwardian working-class life, *The Ragged Trousered Philanthropists*.

For each of those who died there were many more made ill or incapacitated by the same dangers. Little is known in detail about the frequency of illness or its effects on the ability to work. Accidents were better recorded: 'Between 1868 and 1919 a miner was killed every six hours, seriously injured every two hours and injured badly . . . every two or three minutes.'[21] One study of a single Scottish coal mine found that 19 workers were killed and 1,252 injured in a three-year period in 1906–1909, with the average absence from work being two to six weeks; the main cause was falls of coal from the face, but coal wagons were very dangerous. Throughout industry, explosions of the boilers in steam engines seem to have been common. Even in the jute textile industry, one firm with about 2,500 workers recorded one death but 305 injuries in 1897–1901, mostly caused by men and women catching their hands in the machinery, which could often lead to amputation. Even as late as the First World War, machinery was still being cleaned while it was in motion.[22]

Hard work and excessive hours sapped strength even when they did not lead to obvious effects; as one doctor who had studied child labour in factories observed in 1832: '. . . the injury to the general health is of more consequence than any particular deformities.'[23] The point was put more sharply by a factory operative, giving evidence to the same enquiry: 'The doctors may examine one man and may examine another man; but, I would say, look . . . at the gentlemen's sons, and show me the proportion of the knock-knee'd and the deformed that there is among us.'[24]

There is much anecdotal evidence, from sources such as novels, about the incidence of disease and its effects, but it is difficult from this to gauge how often men and women were so ill that they could not work and therefore could not earn. Studies of relatively well-paid and probably relatively healthy engineering workers suggest that, on average, 2.5 per cent of the workforce was ill at any one time throughout the century.[25] In addition, many of the diseases which produced high occupational mortality were insidious and slow to take effect. While fishermen might drown and railway workers be killed in shunting accidents, file makers died from respiratory diseases, chimney sweeps and mule spinners from cancer. All could take years to develop and further years to kill, with the victim increasingly enfeebled and his or her earnings falling. Illness caused the loss on average of 1.7 weeks' work each year for each person employed in British industry in 1913, at the end of a period of improving health, so it seems likely that it was a much more serious cause of loss, to the worker and to the economy, in earlier years.[26]

Illness and its accompaniments, debility and exhaustion, must have been a constant feature of life for many. Less constant, but still very serious in its consequences, was unemployment. On average throughout the period between 1857 and 1913, 4.4 per cent of male workers were unemployed and even at the peaks of the trade cycle unemployment remained above 2 per cent. At the troughs, unemployment could reach 10 per cent; although such a figure has been exceeded for long periods in the late twentieth century, it meant, then as now, waste and misery.

In some areas of work, of course, underemployment was universal, even in boom years; in dock-labour and the building trades large parts of the workforce were casual, employed, if at all, only by the day. So too were many jobs such as porters and carriers. The author's grandparents recalled returning from their honeymoon in 1910 to St Pancras Station in London, to be met by a crowd of boys offering to load their luggage onto a cab; once done, the same boys ran behind the cab to Hampstead, a distance of three miles, to compete for the chance of unloading the luggage from cab to house. Much agricultural work, particularly for women, was equally casual, while across a wide range of occupations workers could be hired by the day or even the hour.

Even in agriculture, where jobs were somewhat more secure, and where it was customary for a house to be provided, men and women like those in Thomas Hardy's *Tess of the d'Urbervilles* had to compete for work on a yearly basis at the hiring fairs for farm servants which were held across the country each Michaelmas. In manufacturing industry, even highly skilled jobs were not immune to rapid changes in fortune. In the engineering industry, for example, where workers had served a seven-years apprenticeship to develop their skills, it was the custom in the 1890s that a man could be hired or fired, without any compensation, at any meal break. In almost all trades, labour costs formed a very high proportion of the costs of any business and the immediate reaction to a downturn in demand was to dismiss workers. An extreme example was the 'cotton famine' created in Lancashire in the early 1860s by the American Civil War, when tens of thousands of workers and their families were thrown upon the Poor Law, but lay-offs or short-term working were commonplace in all industries. Seasons and the weather could play a part; while water power continued to be important, as it was well into the second half of the nineteenth century, work could be interrupted, and men dismissed, during dry summers; indeed, an important contribution of the steam engine, as late as the 1850s, was to substitute for water power at such times.

Once unemployed, only a tiny proportion of workers could rely on support. Some trade unions gave assistance to their members to find work, producing the so-called 'tramping artisans', but this was of little use to men with wives and families, who were soon forced back onto charity or the dreaded Poor Law. For those without dependants, neither the Poor Law nor charity was likely to be available and, for young men, one of the few alternatives was enlistment in the army. Military recruiters were well aware that unemployment was the best inducement for a man to 'take the Queen's shilling'; in 1861 a Royal Commission commented that 'Enlistment is, for the most part, occasioned by want of work' and found that it was particularly easy to get recruits from the agricultural districts in winter, when there were no casual jobs to be had. As late as 1904, another enquiry commented that '. . . we must remember that strikes and things of that kind give us a lot of recruits. . . . We all know that strikes do us a lot of good.'[27]

Single women had no chance to enlist. For them, particularly if they had 'lost their character' through some fault perceived by a previous employer, there were only a range of casual jobs or, at worst, prostitution which, like the Army, tended to recruit well in times of unemployment. But the frequent fictional character of the housemaid turned away without a reference has a wider application to Victorian and Edwardian society. The level of unemployment and the precariousness of employment gave enormous power to the employer. When this was combined with the fact that the society was hierarchical, status-conscious, and organized through a set of often unwritten rules as to what constituted respectable or acceptable behaviour, the worker had to be ever-fearful of transgressing one of those rules and of being disgraced, forced out of employment, and, therefore, losing both self-respect and the respect of friends and neighbours. Even worse, until the passage of the Master and Servant Act in 1867, an employee who broke his contract, for example by striking, was liable to criminal prosecution and penalties; the employer, on the other hand, could only be sued in the civil courts.

Members of the middle class were certainly not free from risk and uncertainty. For a small proportion of the middle and upper classes, living on inherited wealth invested principally in 'the Funds', as fixed-interest Government securities were known, there were few risks of losing their wealth in an era of low or non-existent inflation. A favourite form of savings, even for members of the middle class on relatively low incomes, was to invest in residential property, letting it out for rent; this too gave security and the prospect of modest gains in value.

But for anyone in business the risks were real. Even in the boom of the 1850s, Manchester businessmen 'cannot for long have been free from the fear of commercial collapse lurking behind each temporary revival of trade.'[28] Before 1855 the privilege of limited liability was confined to investors in railways and some chartered companies trading overseas. For everyone else, to set up in business was to risk all one's assets and, moreover, to be fully responsible for the actions of any partner in the business. Many businesses were established despite this, but many failed, carrying their owners into bankruptcy; there were, for example, 1,906 bankruptcies in Britain in 1870, with a total debt of £8,937,000 against assets of £2,400,000. At the depths of the Depression in 1893, the number reached 5,161, with total liabilities of £9,449,000 against assets of £3,251,000.[29] Bankruptcy carried draconian penalties of the loss of almost all possessions, if not by this time the incarceration in debtors' prisons which was possible as late as 1869.

Even if businesses and their owners were not driven into bankruptcy, the chances of survival for a new business appear to have been small. Statistics are difficult to obtain, since many businesses never attained a sufficient size to attract attention or to require any formal registration. But a study of firms making machine tools, a vital sector of the engineering industry and one which required substantial capital in the form of machinery and buildings, found that on average 7 per cent of all firms in the industry disappeared in each year in the 1880s, and 10 per cent of all firms each year in the 1890s.[30] It seems likely that turnover would have been much higher in many industries where there were lower capital requirements to begin at all, such as many other branches of manufacturing and particularly retailing. In such trades, the worker might need only his tools to set up in business on his own, but had no savings to tide him over bad times. It remains true that many new firms were founded each year in all these areas, so that the total number of firms continued to grow along with the economy as a whole, but few firms could feel secure. One source of difficulty even for the larger firms was the insecurity of the banking system, at least at the beginning of the period before the Bank of England developed its role as 'lender of last resort'. But even late in the century, bank failures occurred regularly.

In many cases, insecurity stemmed from lack of information. Accounting practices improved during the century, partly in response to some major frauds and business collapses, but such progress, although it did something to safeguard the shareholders of limited companies established after 1855, was of interest only to a small number of the largest firms. It is true that firms did not have to cope with the late twentieth-century problem of rapidly changing prices and interest rates, which make it difficult to forecast income and expenditure. For most of the period, prices were stable or falling although short-term interest rates, which a businessman might have to pay to finance his work, did vary to some extent during the course of the business cycle, reaching a minimum of 0.96 per cent per annum in 1895 but a maximum of 7.0 per cent in 1864. A more serious source of uncertainty, however, was the difficulty of obtaining good market information; this was particularly so in overseas markets, in an age before the telegraph, the telephone, or the development of methods of market research. Sea transport, whether along the coasts or further afield, continued to be time-consuming and, despite the advent of steamships and the efforts of Samuel Plimsoll, dangerous for crews and the cargoes which they carried.

Guarding against risk

Was it possible to guard against the myriad risks which life and work brought to the men and women of Victorian and Edwardian Britain? In essence, the answer is no. In limited ways, the development of insurance gave some protection; even in 1868 it could be said by a writer in *Belgravia* that 'the community have a general and indistinct notion that all kinds of things can be insured and all kinds of contingencies provided for by paying a certain sum of money yearly or half-yearly into an office.'[31] Risks from fire could easily be covered and in the commercial sphere it was possible to insure against the loss, for example, of a ship at sea. By the 1860s as much as two-thirds of the nation's insurable property was covered by fire insurance.[32]

Life insurance had been developed in various forms in the eighteenth century, essentially as a form of long-term gambling or speculation, and early in the nineteenth century served only a small fraction of the population, principally from the middle and upper classes. From the 1830s, however, there was a dramatic increase and annual expenditure on premiums rose threefold between 1837 and 1870. As the industry grew, it became more sophisticated in the assessment of risk, so that insurance premiums for equivalent risks were little different in the late nineteenth century from those charged today.[33] The British middle classes embraced, far more than was the case in other European countries, the virtues of thrift and independence which were embodied in 'making proper provision'. The development of endowment insurance as a form of savings added to this trend. Insurance could also be used in business transactions, as security for a loan or as protection against the loss of a business partner.[34] From the 1870s, too, insurance extended into new fields: railway accidents, theft, professional liability, and, later, motor and aeroplane insurance. The Acts which, gradually, made employers liable to compensate workers for accidents at work created their own demand for liability insurance.

Life insurance for the working classes in the middle of the nineteenth century did not exist except in the form of burial clubs where tiny sums, put by over many years, would protect against a pauper's funeral. Such insurance was often organized through friendly societies, which provided also social contacts and a sense of respectability; as such, and because of the payments required, they appealed mainly to skilled workers, who gained from them 'the relations of brotherhood, not merely as regards the working of a money insurance scheme, but as regards his whole life and conduct.'[35] By 1872 such societies, including burial societies, were thought to have over 4 million members.[36] But, although by 1912 premiums of £16 million annually were being paid to industrial life assurance societies, the 'Pru' (Prudential) being the dominant office, most were for sums of £10 or less to cover funeral expenses and did not give any substantial security. Employers were, it is true, liable to compensate workers for accidents at work from the 1880s, but this did little to make up for the loss of a livelihood. The illness of the main wage earner could be, for many working-class families, a disaster. This accounts for the growth, again through the agency of friendly societies, of sickness insurance, providing not only payment for the doctor but a small weekly income during sickness.

To many, the search for security became grounds for taking a risk. Gambling, previously tolerated by the law as an eccentricity of the rich, expanded and came to be seen by middle-class Christians in the late nineteenth century as a major social evil. Working-class betting, described by Ramsay MacDonald, later the first Labour Prime Minister, as 'a disease which spreads downwards to the industrious poor from the idle rich' thrived with the development of illegal off-course bookmaking on horse racing, the product of marrying the technology of the telegraph with the development of racing newspapers. The decline in working hours and the rise in disposable incomes helped to fuel the fire.[37]

There were other stratagems for survival. It was important to make use of social networks for mutual benefit, providing paid or unpaid services as part of a reciprocal network of relatives and neighbours. The women of the working classes in particular had to become expert at seizing every opportunity to increase the family income, organizing the labour of children, earning small sums by outwork, 'providing lodgings, taking in washing, child-minding, nursing the sick, attending childbirth and laying out the dead.'[38] Diversification of the sources of family income gave some protection against illness or unemployment. But the major problem for the bulk of the population was that poverty made it impossible to insure against poverty. The risks were so great, and the incomes so small, that hope and prayer were the only possible reactions to the dangers of everyday life.

Risk and rules

A chapter about risk is inevitably pathological; it has to examine the dangers which were inherent in the Victorian and Edwardian economy and society, at the least as a counterweight to the growth which undoubtedly took place in average incomes—and thus in average well-being—that was described in the last chapter. That improvement was real and it made Britain one of the richest societies in the world. People had more money in their pockets, better houses in which to live, for a few, even some savings.

But this was, nevertheless, an age of insecurity which, perhaps as a reaction, emphasized rules which bound men and women into their place in society. Infringement of those rules, whether it be the terrible social solecism for a middle-class man of appearing in the street without a hat—and, moreover, the correct hat for the occasion—or the equal stigma attached to the wife of a clerk who did not keep the front step reddened, or the much more serious misdemeanours of drink, adultery, illegitimacy, or crime, could bring ostracism from the social group, unemployment, and eventually, perhaps, destitution.

For most, failure remained a fear, a horror even, rather than a reality. But the need to demonstrate success and to ward off failure could colour many aspects of life. Dress was a particular mark of status and had to conform, for the sake of respectability, to the social class of the wearer. Sexual scandal must not be created by promiscuity and should never, particularly for the upper classes, become widely known. Nor too, for the middle and upper classes, could public drinking of alcohol be tolerated; the pub was for the working class, while gentlemen had their clubs or drank in moderation at home. Within the home, elaborate rules of etiquette were observed by all social classes, from the upper and middle classes dressing for dinner in full evening dress to the superior working classes with their lace curtains, 'Sunday best' clothing, and the parlour set aside for use only on Sundays.

Lady Wilde, whose son Oscar clearly inherited his gift for a phrase, once commented that 'It is only tradespeople who are respectable; we are above respectability.' But, for most people, the key moral concepts were deference, respectability, and independence. Deference meant 'knowing one's place' but also maintaining or if possible bettering one's place by a well-judged lifestyle. Central to that lifestyle, and to both self-respect and the respect of others, was living within one's means, depending neither on credit or on charity, and displaying prudence. It was particularly imprudent, and could put social position at risk, to marry without the means of supporting a family. Independence was a moral imperative; it was immoral to rely on someone else, so dependence was disreputable and charitable assistance became judgmental, disciplinary, and condescending. It was always difficult to be respectable if you were poor and, at the extreme, the Poor Law with its workhouse, increasingly designed like a prison, emphasized the price of failure.

3

POPULATION CHANGE

The overall course of population change

At the start of the nineteenth century, the growth of population was something to be feared. Under the influence of the Revd Thomas Malthus, who believed that population was increasing and was likely to continue to increase more rapidly than 'the means of subsistence', some observers anticipated famines or epidemics which would provide a 'positive check' as agriculture proved to be unable to feed more and more mouths. Others, more optimistic, hoped for a 'preventive check' whereby later and fewer marriages and sexual abstinence within marriage would limit the number of children being born. Both groups were alarmed by the evidence of their eyes, confirmed by the censuses of the population which were taken in 1801 and then in every tenth year after 1831, that the population was increasing and driving up the size of the cities.

By the middle of the century, despite the Irish potato famine of 1846–50, which was seen by some as the predicted 'positive check' to Irish population growth, the influence of Malthus had waned. In spite of the continued growth of the population, at rates only slightly less rapid than before, it was seen to be providing not only more workers but also more consumers for industry and commerce. In other words, economic growth had come to the rescue; although the population continued to rise, even if at a diminishing rate, early fears of its producing starvation or revolution now seemed entirely fanciful. Attention turned away from the size of the population and towards its condition.

What was the nature of the increase in population between 1831 and 1911, shown in Figure 3.1? Recent discussion of demographic change, based largely on the experience of underdeveloped countries in the twentieth century, has often centred on what is known as the 'demographic transition.' According to this model or framework of analysis, pre-industrial societies have birth and death rates which are both high. In other words, many children are born but their numbers are roughly balanced by the number of children and adults who die. The population is thus stable despite a high birth rate, kept high by the lack of contraception, the will to reproduce, and the need to have children to keep their parents in old age.

During a demographic transition from such a position, the birth rate may increase slightly, but the most influential change is a fall in the death rate, perhaps brought about by the declining impact of epidemic disease or by increased incomes associated with industrialization or a boost in agricultural production. The conjunction of a stable or rising birth rate with a declining death rate produces rapid population increase. After a time, however, parents begin to realize that more children are surviving to

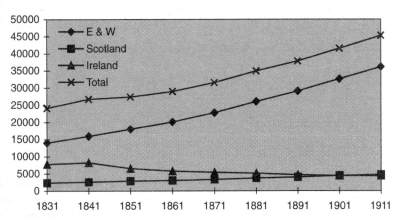

FIG. 3.1   Population of the United Kingdom, 1831–1911 ('000s)

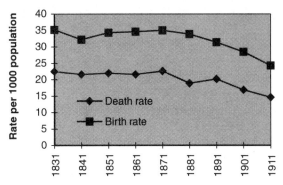

FIG. 3.2   Fertility and Mortality in England and Wales, 1831–1911

adulthood and that fewer children need to be born; the birth rate then falls and the demographic transition is complete, with a stable population now produced by low birth and death rates.

Unfortunately, as Figure 3.2 shows, the British experience was not at all like that; almost no aspect of the demographic transition model applies to Britain. But the model does focus attention on the important variables, factors which changed during the period: they are the birth rate, the marriage rate, the death rate and, of increasing importance as the nineteenth century wore on, the migration rate. All of them were greatly influenced by, and they influenced in turn, the state of the economy and society in general. Upon population change depended the number of workers and the number of consumers whose increase underpinned economic growth.

Fertility and nuptiality

In order to understand British population change, it is necessary to begin before 1830. The period between 1826 and 1830 saw the largest percentage growth in the English population of any five-year period in the eighteenth and nineteenth centuries. The year 1830 is, therefore, something of a turning-point, the culmination of over one century of rapid population growth and the beginning of a new phase. That was the situation at least for England and Wales; the other parts of the United Kingdom had different experiences, as will be seen later.

The rapid growth before 1830 was produced almost entirely by increases in fertility which were themselves determined by changes in nuptiality; the growth was not (contrary to the demographic transition model) a result of falling mortality. These technical terms require explanation. First, fertility describes the number of children produced by a population at a particular time, which can be measured either by the crude birth rate (the number of children born in a year per 1,000 members of the population) or by more complex measures such as the gross reproduction rate (the number of female children born to an average woman). Second, nuptiality describes the pairing behaviour of humans; it is measured by the average age at which men and women marry and by the proportion who marry, although it is important not to forget that there were children born from sexual relationships outside marriage. Last, mortality is death; demographers measure it by the crude death rate (the number who die in a year per 1,000 members of the population) or by more complex measures such as the average expectation of life or the infant mortality rate (the number of infants who die per 1,000 live births). To move away from jargon, the first sentence of this paragraph therefore means that more children were born because more women married younger.

Before 1830, the major influence on English population change had, for nearly a century, been a decline in the average age of marriage of women; as seen in a sample of parish registers, that age fell from 26.1 in 1700–24 to 23.2 in 1825–49. The age of marriage of men also changed, but for obvious reasons is of less interest to the study of fertility. There was little change in the proportion of women who married or in the intervals between the births of their children, but the declining age of marriage and therefore the increased length of the childbearing period for women produced a considerable increase in the number of children born within marriage. There was also an increase in the number of children conceived before marriage and a substantial increase in the number of illegitimate children. The overall effect was that, while at the end of the seventeenth century the average woman bore just under two female children (and therefore about four children altogether), by the 1820s this gross reproduction rate was just under three. In other words, the average woman had one-and-a-half times as many children in the 1820s as in 1700.

By 1830, the situation was already changing; the age at marriage of women was rising once again, to an average of 25.8 between 1851 and 1914 which was close to that previously experienced in 1725–49. This brought about a fall in the gross reproduction rate. Couples married in the 1870s still had about six male or female children, but marriages in the 1900s produced about five. The transition to modern levels of fertility in England and Wales was well under way. In Scotland, fertility was stable until the late 1870s, after which it began to decline in the same way as in England. In Ireland, the number of children born to a marriage was always high and, until the Famine of the 1840s, the Irish married early, giving rise to very high overall fertility; after the 1840s, the rate of marriage fell precipitately and, with it, overall fertility to levels well below those in Britain.

This pattern of fertility change prompts two immediate questions: how and why? As to how, artificial methods of birth control were little used before 1914; it is nevertheless clear that the average numbers of children born throughout the period were far below the level of 'natural fertility', estimated as it has been from studies of populations where it is known that no form of fertility control was used. The average age at marriage, which for women always came some years after children could physically be borne, bears some responsibility. It also seems certain that couples, even in the eighteenth century, deliberately spaced their children either by abstinence or by non-mechanical means of birth control. Knowledge of methods of birth control certainly spread at the end of the nineteenth century, although notions that such knowledge was disseminated from the middle to the working classes seem to be too simple. Whatever the method, the important fact is that, whether by changing their age at marriage or by birth control, the English people of the eighteenth and, even more, the nineteenth centuries were able to control their fertility.

'Why?' is much more difficult. First, it seems unlikely that it happened by chance or as a result of the whims of fashion. It is much more likely that young people responded, in fixing their marriages or determining the spacing of their children, to perceptions of what they might be able to afford in setting up households or bringing up children. But such a statement merely underlines the difficulty of establishing the reasons for a myriad decisions based on the standard of living which those young people had or wished to have, the prospects of jobs, the availability of housing, or their judgement of when children could contribute to the family income. There seems, in the eighteenth century, to have been some relationship between rising real wages and rising birth rates, but this broke down after 1830. Nor does it seem likely that the switch to a punitive Poor Law after 1834, although it certainly reduced support for large and poor families, could have affected a sufficient proportion of the population to bring about a change in behaviour, towards lower numbers of children, which lasted for the next century.

Nevertheless, rising incomes and rising consumption, particularly of leisure, seem the most likely explanations for the fall in fertility, as families 'spent' their increased incomes on things rather than children. Fertility is, however, only half the story. Before trying to make progress in explaining population change, it is necessary to consider morbidity and mortality.

Morbidity and mortality

First, another piece of demographers' jargon: morbidity means illness, measured in such ways as the numbers of days lost from work or the incidence of chronic disease among the population. Measured in theory, that is, since evidence on the levels of illness in Victorian and Edwardian England is very defective. A great deal is known about when and where people died; much is known about why they died, particularly as medical knowledge and diagnostic skill improved in the course of time, but much less can be discovered from medical records about the state of health of the population.

It is fortunate, therefore, that the average height of a population, or of sub-groups within a population, gives a very precise guide to what is called the 'nutritional status' of that population or sub-group. Nutritional status is a term which includes more than nutrition or food intake; it describes the balance between the intake of nutrients, warmth and housing, and even, possibly, the love and affection received by a child, on the one hand and, on the other, the energy needed to exist, to work, or to fight disease. If a child has a positive energy balance, it can grow to its full potential; if not, it will be stunted. Average height changes, therefore, in response to alterations in the standard of living and state of health of the population in its early years, particularly in the two or three years after birth.

The evidence of height statistics, derived mainly from measurements made of recruits to the armed forces, is difficult to interpret. But what it seems to show is that average heights of groups of young men in Britain and Ireland increased for about fifty years, from those born in the 1780s up to the group born around 1830, but that heights then declined for a period of about thirty years; growth resumed with young men born in the 1860s and 1870s and then continued into the twentieth century.[1] This suggests that the urban environment, in which an increasing proportion of the population lived, and where disease levels were high, was adversely affecting the health of the population before the 1870s. This is despite the fact that other measures of well-being, such as real wages, suggest that in other respects the standard of living was improving at the time.

The ultimate evidence, of death itself, confirms the view that there was only a very gradual improvement to health in the years immediately after 1830. Since as death rates fall people live longer, the most convenient and evocative overall indicator of mortality is the average expectation of life, shown in Figure 3.3. If, in each year, 5 per cent of the population were to die, then on average each person would live for $100/5 = 20$ years and average

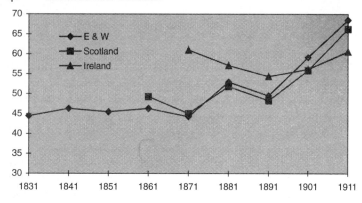

FIG. 3.3   Expectation of life at birth, United Kingdom 1831–1911

life expectation would be 20 years. In the first half of the eighteenth century the average person in England and Wales lived for between 35 and 40 years, although there were quite strong fluctuations in mortality and thus in expectation of life from year to year as a result of epidemic disease. After 1750 expectation of life crept upwards, at the same time as mortality became more stable, to reach a level of just over 45 in the 1830s. Thereafter the improvement continued at a very gradual rate for a period of 70 years, before death rates began to fall rapidly at the beginning of the twentieth century. (A different method of calculating life expectancy, from the average age of those who died in a particular year, gives lower figures, but the same pattern of change.) By 1911 the expectation of life at birth in England and Wales was 68 years. Today it is over 85 years.

Once again, it is important to note that mortality in Scotland and Ireland was at different levels, and changed in different ways, from the experience in England and Wales. In Scotland, the growth of the towns and cities produced an increase in mortality, probably from epidemic disease, which seems to have been more marked than was the case in England and Wales, although it responded by the end of the century to improvements in public health. In Ireland, by contrast, it was the rural areas which bore the brunt of the Famine of 1846 to 1848, a demographic event which was unprecedented and unparalleled in modern European history. The Irish economy was not integrated with that of Britain and, by the early decades of the nineteenth century, was experiencing deindustrialization or the loss of manufacturing industry, for example in textiles, while the English and Scottish economies were expanding rapidly. Irish agriculture was, by that period, dominated by relatively small holdings, dependent largely on potatoes, both as a cash crop and for sale. The potato blight which spread across Ireland in 1846 left much of the agricultural community without their basic food and without the money to buy anything else, while the remainder of the economy was too weak to bear the burden. The British government's efforts at relief were wholly inadequate and between 1 and 1.5 million people died.

What were the main determinants of changes in mortality? As the experience of Scotland and Ireland demonstrates vividly, there was a strong regional impact on death, which varied and changed over time. Second, the pattern of deaths by age also changed greatly between 1830 and 1914, although it is complicated to describe in detail. Moreover, these two factors interacted with each other.

Victorian cities were unhealthy and to live in them rather than in the country increased the chance of death of both child and adult. The larger and more densely populated the city, the more unhealthy it was. In 1831, for example, people who died in London had lived on average 32 years, those who died in another town or city of over 100,000 inhabitants 31 years, and those who died in a town with between 10,000 and 100,000 people 35 years. All these life expectations were lower than the national average of 40 years because it was healthier to live, as most did, in the country; those who died there had lived on average for 43 years.

As towns and cities grew, more and more people were exposed to urban death rates; in 1831 only 34 per cent of the population of England and Wales lived in towns or cities of more than 10,000 people, but by 1911 this proportion was 70 per cent.

So, although both town and country gradually became healthier places in which to live and the difference between them lessened, the national average was slow to improve. By 1911, however, the towns were almost as healthy and the country only slightly more healthy than the average.

These averages are, however, deceptive in a second way. In 1831 and for most of the nineteenth century, as in the underdeveloped world today, babies struggled to survive their first year of life and, until about 1900, 150 in every 1,000 lost the struggle. After 1900, infant mortality declined rapidly. By the time of the First World War, about 100 in every 1,000 babies died; this was still a terrible toll by the standards of the late twentieth century, when only about 12 in every 1,000 die, but improvement it was. It is clear however that the slow rise in life expectancy before 1900 cannot have been produced by an improvement in the survival of infants. It stemmed largely, in fact, from a decline in deaths among those aged 1–14, beginning in the 1860s and from a decline in deaths among those aged 15–44, beginning in the 1870s.

Why did all these different and complex changes in patterns of death occur? It is tempting, and strictly correct, to say that no one really knows, despite many decades of historical research and analysis. Logically, there are five possible explanations: first, the diseases which killed men, women, and children in the early nineteenth century could have changed in character and become less virulent; second, medical treatments of those diseases could have improved; third, public health measures could have improved the environment; fourth, nutritional status could have improved and brought increased resistance to disease; last, and most likely, a combination of these possibilities could have occurred.

It does not seem that either changing diseases or better medicine played much of a role. The old calumny that people actually increased their chance of death by entering a nineteenth-century hospital has been disproved, but none of the medical or drug therapies which later treated almost all the killer diseases of the nineteenth century—tuberculosis, scarlet fever, whooping

cough, diphtheria, pneumonia, cholera, typhoid, and typhus—
were developed in time to affect the mortality decline. Only
smallpox yielded to vaccination.

It is possible that the diseases themselves altered in character,
but more likely that the ability of humans to combat them was
enhanced. This is implied by the little evidence which exists from
the records of friendly societies about the incidence of disease
which did not lead to death; it seems that, as death rates fell
towards the end of the century, the length of illnesses increased,
implying that the conditions causing disease were still extant but
that they could be overcome. As Riley puts it in his study of the
friendly society of Odd Fellows: 'Mortality declined not because
the risk of falling sick declined—that is, not because the Odd
Fellows were exposed to fewer diseases—but because the sick-
nesses they did experience were resolved less frequently in
death. . . . Morbidity increased because mortality decreased.'[2]
However, this conclusion is based on the experience of relatively
small numbers and there are examples to the contrary; engineering workers did not show any marked increase in morbidity.[3]

Public health measures were certainly taken and some historians have argued that their importance was great.[4] Following a
series of reports on the health of the population produced by
Edwin Chadwick in the 1840s, the burial of bodies in urban areas
was regulated and work was put in hand to improve the water
supplies and sewerage systems. The invention of the water closet
combined with improvements to drains to put an end to open
sewers, although even Buckingham Palace still had untrapped
drains in mid-century and the smell of sewage pervaded the
royal apartments. Such measures did a great deal to lessen the
impact and restrict the spread of water-borne diseases such as
cholera, typhoid, and diarrhoea. Food and drink became purer
as a result of legislation affecting additives and the new technologies of refrigeration and, at the turn of the century, pasteuri-
zation of milk.

It seems likely, however, that the major influence on mortality
was an improvement in nutritional status. This is a controversial
topic among historians, partly because it was difficult until re-

cently to obtain direct evidence about the nutritional status of the population; those who argued for its importance were forced instead to attack other possible explanations. The new evidence of changing heights provides such direct evidence, even if there is still room for debate about the timing of improvements and about why infant mortality did not improve until early in the twentieth century. But the link between better nutrition and greater resistance to disease is so well-attested in the developing world today that there is little room for doubt as to the overall reason for falling mortality, especially as so many of the diseases of the nineteenth century which have now largely disappeared in Britain—tuberculosis is the main example—are known to be best combated by better nutrition. Despite the numbers still living in poverty, the average increase of 3.3 times in British incomes bought longer lives for the people.

Migration

Many people believe that men and women in the nineteenth and earlier centuries spent most of their lives close to the place in which they had been born; but this is a myth. Even in the eighteenth century, a large proportion of young men and women left home during adolescence to work in other households away from their own town or village and three out of four, when they married, set up households in a village different from that in which they had been brought up. By 1851, 54 per cent of the population were living over 2 km. from their birthplaces. The improvement in transport during the nineteenth century only made this easier; the bicycle certainly had a substantial impact on rural courtship.

It was, however, the growth of towns and cities which provided the major stimulus to the movement of people in the nineteenth and early twentieth centuries, although migration overseas became of increasing importance. In both cases, although individual motivations were no doubt complex and various, migration was largely stimulated by the wish to improve economic circumstances—in incomes or in prospects—itself fired by a greater and greater flow of information from those who had gone before.

Within Britain, the towns and cities grew predominantly by natural increase—the birth of children to those already living there—but they also attracted very large numbers of migrants from the countryside, including the countryside of Ireland. The movement was certainly not all one way; there is much evidence of migrants returning to their birthplaces, after a spell perhaps as a domestic servant in a town. Much migration was short-term or even seasonal in character, even over quite long distances. The larger towns such as London, Liverpool, Leeds, Manchester, Birmingham, and Glasgow, as one might expect because they provided more jobs, drew migrants from longer distances than did the smaller towns where migrants came particularly from the surrounding countryside. This is a natural result of flows of information; news of the larger cities and of the opportunities in them spreads more widely than does news of smaller towns and there were also more previous migrants in the big cities to write home about the 'streets paved with gold'.

As a result, migrants to the cities did not necessarily come from the poorest rural areas; they came from all parts of Britain and Ireland. Between 1841 and 1911 the British countryside lost more than 4.5 million people and another 1 million left Ireland for British cities. Probably less than half had previously worked in agriculture, so that the majority had experience either of domestic service or of the many rural trades, such as lace-making, straw-plaiting, or ribbon-making, which were supplanted or replaced by urban manufacturing. It is thus wrong to think of migrants as farm labourers displaced from the land and thrust into the alien environment of the factory; although some may have chosen to make such a move, for the vast majority the change would have been less violent and certainly more voluntary, perhaps the culmination of a period of moving from place to place seeking a job. Nor were migrants typically to be found alone in the city, with no friends or relatives to care for them; people sought help where they could find it in their new environment, perhaps seeking lodging at first with someone originally from their own village. This was most marked, or perhaps most obvious, among the Irish; half of the first-generation migrants from Ireland to Britain lived in London, Manchester, Glasgow, and Liverpool and clustered together even within those cities.

More concentrated again were the only sizeable group of immigrants to Britain from overseas, the Jewish migrants from eastern Europe, about 120,000 of whom came to Britain between 1880 and the First World War. Three-quarters settled in London, the vast majority working in the single trade of clothing manufacture. Like most immigrant groups, they were at first the object of racist attacks and of fears that they were contributing to urban degeneration, but numerically they were always a tiny part of the population even of the cities in which they lived. They were greatly outnumbered, also, by those born in Britain who sailed to live overseas.

The amount of emigration from Britain, particularly Scotland, and from Ireland, is one of the most striking features of the economic history of the period, unsurpassed either before 1830 or after 1914 and hardly rivalled by other countries at the time or since. Between 1853 and 1910 over 6,500,000 people left England and Wales for non-European destinations and several million more from Ireland and Scotland. Despite the waves of emigration from Eastern and Mediterranean Europe, it is likely that Scotland and Ireland lost more of their populations through emigration than did any other western European country at the time. The most popular destination was the United States, followed by Canada and Australia. This immense movement of people was by no means continuous; there were periods when migration was a flood, at others a trickle, as migrants balanced the attractions of the economy abroad against those of the economy at home. The peak decade was that of the 1880s. Nor was migration always for life; perhaps as many as half returned sooner or later to Britain. Emigrants were counterbalanced by immigrants from the rest of Europe, but the loss of population from Britain was 2,160,000 between 1861 and 1911, with a further 860,000 leaving between 1911 and 1921, most of them before 1914.[5] Perhaps the most dramatic of these population movements, however, was that from Ireland after the Famine, much of it to Scotland but also to the United States and other countries of white settlement.

One speaks of a 'loss' of population, but it is doubtful whether anyone, whether the men or (fewer) women who left or the country as a whole, should have been regretful. Migration was a continuum; it ranged, seamlessly, from the young woman who left her family to become a maid in the great house in the next village to the old man who left England for Australia to join his children there. Britain, Ireland, the United States, and the countries of white settlement in the British Empire formed essentially a single labour market, through which men and women moved in response to hopes and fears and to information which was no doubt often misleading, optimistic, or out of date; but overall it worked well. The leading historian of emigration, Dudley Baines, wrote: 'In the main, the emigrants were not fleeing from problems at home nor were they going blindly overseas. Most of the English and Welsh emigrants of the later nineteenth century must have been going to parts of the world which they knew something about.'[6] Even more was this true of the migrant from country to country town, but the motives were much the same. Many must have been disappointed but most were satisfied. For the economies of Britain and other countries, it was certainly better to have a population which was ready to move and to adapt to new circumstances and new demands.

Why?

Explaining the course of population change between 1830 and 1914, or indeed in any period, may seem an impossible task. The size of a population is determined by a variety of individual decisions, some voluntary or semi-voluntary, like marriage or the bearing of children, some involuntary, like illness or death. Yet human behaviour is not random; it follows patterns. Individuals respond in similar ways to the environment in which they live, to its history, its culture, and the expectations of others. Thus the decision whether or not to have another child was taken by each couple but it was affected, whether each man or woman realized it or not, by factors which were, at the same time, influencing many other couples to take the same decision. Similarly, individual behaviour which could increase or diminish the chances of illness or death could be learned, transmitted from one person to another, and, in aggregate, could affect rates of morbidity and mortality.

In such ways, the British population between 1830 and 1914 responded to its improved standard of living, itself brought about by economic growth, and to changing institutions or economic rules which British society developed for itself. Changes in the nature of the labour market, increasing controls on child labour, and an increased emphasis, ultimately backed by law, on the benefits of education together raised the costs and reduced the financial benefit of having children. Declining child death rates gave a greater confidence that children would survive; it was no longer likely that all the children in a family would die, leaving their parents bereft and unsupported. Economic growth thus reduced the need to have children just at the time that adults were living longer; they gained the benefit in health and longevity of earlier economic growth and, because they were healthier and lived longer, they could in their turn contribute to continuing that growth. The pattern of population change was, in other words, bound up in the pattern of economic change.

4

HOUSEHOLDS AND COMMUNITIES

Households and their houses

Britain in the late twentieth century faces, with some trepidation, an ageing of the population; Britain in the early nineteenth century experienced a 'youthing' of the population. Despite deaths in infancy, the high birth rates before 1830 produced a large number of children and young people in the population; as Figure 4.1 shows, between 1841 and 1911, while these children and young people grew up, the proportion of the population aged 15–59 rose from 59.5 per cent to 64.2 per cent in England and Wales and from 59.0 per cent to 62.3 per cent in Scotland. All those men and women worked or were available for work and almost all got married and had children. Their work is discussed later; here the focus is on the households which they formed. Because the population was young and growing, as a result of the high birth rates of earlier generations, the number of marriages rose from an average of 110,000 each year in the 1830s to an average of 263,000 each year between 1900 and 1909.

By and large, each of these marriages meant the formation of a separate household, with separate requirements for housing, household equipment, and furniture. Young married couples in Victorian and Edwardian Britain did not, in general, live with parents or in-laws or at least they did so to a much smaller extent than became common in the twentieth century. This was not, as might be thought, a change from earlier periods, for researchers have failed to identify any period of British history, at least since the sixteenth century, in which people in Britain lived in the

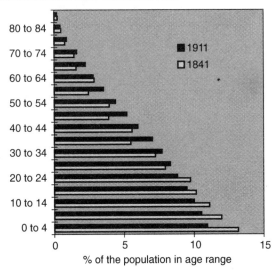

FIG. 4.1   The age distribution of the population of Britain, 1841–1911

large households which were characteristic of some other European societies. Britain was the land of the nuclear family and household, and in 1851 only 6.3 per cent of the population were living as relatives in someone else's house. Households were more complex than at the end of the twentieth century in two different ways: first, more had living-in servants, 16 per cent of households in 1851, and many more had lodgers, 12 per cent of households in 1851. Both had become less common by 1914.

More households meant more housing. The housing market in Britain in the nineteenth century was far more flexible than it became, under the influence of rent control on tenancies and the move towards owner-occupation, in the years after the First World War. Almost everyone lived in rented accommodation; there were some survivals, principally in agriculture and in mining, of the older pattern in which housing had been provided by employers, but the vast majority of the population had to find their own housing. From the 1850s onwards, a few benevolent employers, such as Titus Salt at Saltaire, George Cadbury at

Bournville, and Lord Leverhulme at Port Sunlight, built model villages for their workforce, but these were very much the exception. Rented accommodation, on weekly tenancies, meant everything from a share of a rented room up to the large houses of the middle class. This flexibility was necessary in a situation where so many lived close to the margin and where housing represented, for the working class, the largest single item in their weekly expenditure.

Even if the first home for many newly-married couples was a single rented room, the cumulative demand for housing which stemmed from the rising population and the growing number of marriages was very substantial; it was a major influence on the state of the economy. For much of the nineteenth century wages rose more rapidly than rents and it seems that some at least of the benefit was taken in the form of more and better housing. In England and Wales the 1851 census recorded the existence of 4,432,000 houses but by 1911 this had risen to 7,550,000; in Scotland, 799,000 houses in 1881 increased to 1,102,000 in 1911. There was some demolition of older property, to clear some of the worst slums and to allow for the construction of railways, offices, and factories but new building far more than compensated; there were only three years between 1856 and 1911 in which fewer than 50,000 houses were actually built. In seventeen of those years the number built rose over 100,000 and it never fell below that figure between 1896 and 1908, the period of a major boom in building; the peak was reached with the construction of 157,700 houses in 1898.[1]

Building and furnishing homes was, therefore, a major part of economic activity, both as consumption (defined as expenditure on goods with a life of less than one year) and as investment (defined as expenditure on goods, sometimes called durable goods, with a life of longer than one year). In 1856, for example, £6 million was spent on the construction of dwellings, out of total capital expenditure—on ships, vehicles, equipment, and machinery and buildings of all kinds—of £40 million. In 1899, at the height of the building boom, the investment was £38 million from total capital expenditure of £199 million. In other words, between 15 and 20 per cent of all capital expenditure within Britain went on private housing (although the percentage would be lower if capital expenditure by the British abroad were included). In addition, of course, money was spent each year on furniture and furnishings, cooking equipment, household textiles, and cleaning materials; by 1913, the total spent in this way was £134 million, or 6 per cent of total consumers' expenditure in that year.[2]

All this expenditure did more than keep pace with rising population; it bought an improvement in the nation's housing. The average size of houses increased, they were better furnished and they contained more amenities in the form of sanitary and cooking equipment and luxuries such as pianos. But, as with every other feature of nineteenth-century society, great inequality remained and the standard of amenities, even in 1913, left much to be desired. In 1911, for example, 31.6 per cent of the population of Newcastle was living in overcrowded accommodation, defined as there being more than two persons for each room, while only 1.1 per cent of Leicester's population was in this position. However, everyone in Newcastle had piped water, a great improvement over the 1840s when 'less than one in twelve of the population had access to a piped water supply . . . [or 1883/5, when] 33.1% of households had an indoor and 32.7 per cent an outdoor supply.'[3] There was a similar improvement in sanitary fittings, where water closets largely replaced older forms of sanitation, but most working-class houses in Britain remained without inside toilets even in 1913; Manchester in 1911 had water closets in less than half its houses and the others were still using pail-closets, ash-boxes, ashbins, midden privies, and wet and dry middens.

Whatever the condition of the housing, there is no doubt that, as in the twentieth century, it played a central role in situating the family, and particularly the women, within society. The achievement of more space, perhaps in a better neighbourhood, with more amenities within the house and easier access to parks or shops, was a prize worth scrimping and saving for; once achieved, for example by the family of a skilled worker, it was marked by rituals of care and decoration. What seem today to be minute differences in the style of Victorian and Edwardian houses, for example in the size and patterning of plaster mouldings on the ceilings of rooms, or the quality of ceramic tiles around the fireplace, signified gradations in social status which were of great importance to those who looked at them with pride or envy.

Even more prized, although out of the reach of most, were the suburban houses built from the late Victorian period, culminating in the years before the First World War with the garden cities, such as Letchworth and Welwyn. But gardens, whether attached to a suburban villa or a town house, were an important part of life. To the pitman living in terrace housing, albeit often in semi-rural or village surroundings, in the north-east of England, 'they were places where [he] could establish his own identity, where he could give expression to his own individuality and create' by the growing of flowers, as well as vegetables.[4] To George Cadbury, building his model village at Bournville, gardens were a cure for urban ills, while to the middle classes the villa, hidden behind high garden walls, gave 'privacy to the individual and family, closeness to nature, but a nature safely enclosed by man-made walls, and social exclusiveness.'[5] The moral force of the garden became a theme in Victorian literature.[6]

Gardening became, in fact, an important source of employment—there were 120,000 gardeners employed as domestic servants in 1911—and of consumption expenditure, particularly as interest in it spanned all social classes. Throughout the country, but perhaps particularly in the North of England, local horticultural societies were formed, in the main as organizers of competitions; some plants became the speciality of particular social groups, the weavers of Lancashire, Spitalfields, and West Scotland being responsible for the development of auriculas.[7] Seedsmen and nurserymen flourished; as early as 1826 one London nursery held 1,393 varieties of rose. The Victorians and Edwardians had a voracious appetite for plants, and collecting and propagating for cultivation in gardens great and small were major activities in this period.[8] There was little sign in these rural idylls of the impact of machine civilization, apart from the invention of the lawn mower in 1831, its use being recommended to country gentlemen as 'an amusing, useful, and healthy exercise',[9] but the appearance of gardens changed with the craze for formal flower beds—and, in the 1880s, with the introduction from Germany of the garden gnome.

The growth of the cities

While families increasingly retreated behind their lace curtains from the life of the street which had characterized earlier decades, they could not ignore the world outside their houses; that wider context was increasingly an urban one and the creation of the towns and cities between 1830 and 1914 implied far more even than the building of millions of homes.

Between 1830 and 1911 Britain became an urban nation. At the census of 1831 only 14 per cent of the population lived in large towns and cities of over 50,000 inhabitants. London, with nearly 2 million, was by far the largest city, with over nine times as many people as Glasgow and Liverpool, its two nearest rivals. Five more towns, Birmingham, Bristol, Edinburgh, Leeds, and Manchester, had more than 100,000 people within them and there were a further ten towns with between 50,000 and 100,000 people. The expanding areas of the first part of the century were a mixture of the old regional centres and of market towns which grew together with, in particular, two new groups. These were the towns whose growth and prosperity was based on the textile and metal trades—St Helens, Burnley, Bradford, and others in Lancashire, Yorkshire, and the West Midlands—and the middle-class resorts, with a prosperity based on leisure—Brighton, Cheltenham, Hastings, Torquay. There had also been some growth of smaller towns around London.

By 1911, by contrast, 42 per cent of the British population lived in towns or cities of more than 50,000 people. The major growth in the second part of the century had been in the capital goods, machinery and coal, iron and steel areas of South Wales, north-east England, and the West of Scotland. London, with over 4 million, remained predominant and pre-eminent, still nine times larger than Glasgow, which now had more than 500,000 inhabitants, as did Birmingham, Liverpool, and Manchester. There were now thirty-seven towns of between 100,000 and 500,000 people, together with twenty-four more containing over 50,000. Many people, of course, lived in towns of more than 20,000, the modern definition of an urban area.[10]

Very few cities were built from scratch, the result of conscious planning by the local landowners; Middlesbrough, begun in 1830 as an industrial city and port on the Tees, and Eastbourne, laid out in the 1880s and 1890s as a seaside resort and retirement haven, were the exceptions, although others were tried and failed. For the rest, new homes, offices, factories, and workshops were imposed on old patterns of settlement, often at explosive rates of growth of 10 per cent or more each year for some decades. As a result, as in so many cities of the third world in the twentieth century, the infrastructure of the cities—roads, sewers, water supplies, shops, transport networks—came under intense strain as local government and private businessmen struggled to keep up with the pressure of population.

The strain was felt in unexpected areas; Edwin Chadwick, one of the first great social scientists and reformers, documented in 1843 in 'a special enquiry into the practice of interment in towns' the horrible effects of the growth of towns on their ability to bury their dead.[11] But by 1850, when there was another survey of the subject, little had been done to provide new burial grounds; the enquiry found that around Sheffield Parish Church, for example, the graveyard was six feet above the level of the surrounding houses, the soil 'composed almost entirely of decomposed human bodies.'[12] Coffins were piled upon coffins, six or seven in one grave, and the graveyard drained directly into the streets. The smells were so terrible that even doctors fainted. Chadwick recommended as an ideal for town burial grounds that there should be no more than 110 burials each year per acre; he found one in London, owned by an undertaker and used by Dissenters, where 2,300 burials took place in a year per acre and spectators saw 'the heaped soil, saturated and blackened with human remains and fragments of the dead.'[13]

Conditions in the cities altered rapidly for the worse. In Jane Austen's *Emma*, published in 1816, the heroine's father, Mr Woodhouse, is eccentric in his opinion that 'Nobody is healthy in London, nobody can be.' In mid-century, on the other hand, the eminent scientist Michael Faraday described a trip along the Thames: 'The whole of the river was an opaque, pale brown fluid. . . . The smell was very bad, and common to the whole of the water; it was the same as that which now comes up from the gulley holes in the streets; the whole river was for the time a real sewer.'[14] Little was done, and by 1858 the curtains in the Houses of Parliament were being soaked in chloride of lime to try to drown the smell of the river. Even so, Benjamin Disraeli, then Chancellor of the Exchequer, was seen fleeing from the chamber of the House of Commons. He authorized expenditure for the proper drainage of London, which led to the end of what had been known as the 'Great Stink'. In such conditions, it is no wonder that most Victorians were convinced by the 'miasma' theory that disease was the product of foul air.

Industrial activity in the towns and cities was initially uncontrolled and could give rise to major pollution. In 1862 it was found, for example, that Poplar Union in East London contained 58 factories and distilleries which were 'offensive or injurious to health' including 17 making manure from fish and night soil, 10 boiling bones, 5 making varnish, 1 smelting antimony, and 11 manufacturing chemists, whose products included vitriol and hydrochloric acid. The waste products from such urban industry were commonly discharged into rivers or canals; the Royal Commission on the Pollution of Rivers in 1867 found that it was an amusement for boys to 'set the Bradford Canal on fire. . . . the flame rising six feet and running along the water for many yards, like a will-o-the-wisp; canal boats have been so enveloped in flame as to frighten persons on board.'[15]

The growth of towns and cities demanded, and ultimately secured, action of three main kinds. First, houses, factories, shops, and offices were built, largely by private enterprise and often by men in a very small way of business. Second, they were provided with an infrastructure by a mixture of private and, increasingly, public enterprise. Third, they were governed, by public institutions whose authority and activity became, in many places, a matter of intense civic pride and which, particularly towards the end of the century, asserted themselves in opposition to central government in London.

The building of the cities was an immense enterprise. Leone Levi wrote in 1867 of 'houses, churches, hospitals, gaols . . . exhibition buildings and hotels springing up with wonderful speed and in dimensions beyond precedent.'[16] The investment in houses which was described in the last section was great enough, but it was exceeded by investment in other forms of building, of factories, workshops, shops, offices, and public buildings, almost all of it in the towns and cities. In 1856, for example, £6 million was spent on dwellings, but £14 million on the construction of 'other new buildings and works' (including the cost of the land on which they were built). Annual expenditure on non-residential building reached £82 million at the height of the boom in 1903, just over 40 per cent of all capital expenditure undertaken within Britain. While these figures include expenditure on the construction of the rail and tram networks which, particularly in the second half of the century, predominantly served the urban areas, separate spending on railway and tram rolling stock reached £8 million annually by 1900.[17] Putting houses, non-residential building, and transport equipment together, the building and equipping of the cities was then costing each person in Britain £4.75 each year at a time when the gross domestic product per capita (the total value of the output of the British economy divided by the population) was only £43 each year. In other words, over 10 per cent of all activity in the domestic economy was being used to generate this investment.[18]

How was it done? House-building was undertaken largely by a host of small builders who built as a speculation, hoping to sell quickly to pay off debts and to provide capital for the next venture. Most were themselves building craftsmen, who had managed to save small sums or who had access to short-term credit from banks, solicitors, building societies, and insurance companies; they employed people much like themselves as workers and subcontractors.[19] The houses were typically bought by small investors; rental housing was a favourite nest egg of less wealthy savers as a safe and reliable investment, although the law was moving in favour of protecting the rights of tenants against landlords even before the advent of rent control during the First World War.[20] The typical lower-middle-class household sought to accumulate savings from business or profession which, in late middle age, with the children having left home, could be invested in property and particularly housing property over which control and oversight could be exercised. Not for them investment in stocks, shares, or overseas property. As a result, ownership was fragmented; in 1895, Blackburn, a town of 125,000 people, had 3,365 owners of house property, with the largest single owner possessing only 1.1 per cent of all rented property in the town. A government enquiry in 1834 was told that house property was owned by 'generally retired tradesmen, widows, and persons of small property' and this remained true until 1914.[21]

Not all housing investment was of this type; employers provided some housing, charities such as the Peabody Trust, whose buildings can still be seen in London, built particularly for artisans and craftsmen and, finally, local authorities began to build low-cost housing in the years before the First World War. The building society movement, despite some vicissitudes and financial scandals, also played its part. But there was little involvement of large-scale investors or public companies, even in commercial or industrial buildings. Most, increasingly lavish and grandiose as they became in the height of Victorian and Edwardian prosperity, were financed by the firms themselves out of profits. Many remain, especially in London, where head offices such as the Prudential Building in Holborn or hotels at the main railway stations such as the Midland Grand Hotel at St Pancras testify to the desire for display.

Private buildings were, however, only a part of the construction of towns and cities. In order to function, such buildings needed roads, public transport, water supplies, drains, heat, light, and power supplies, police stations, hospitals, schools, and those glories of English and Scottish municipal architecture, the town halls from which the increasingly self-confident local authorities directed affairs. In many towns and cities, it was first necessary to disentangle the maze of local responsibilities, sometimes dating back to late medieval times, and to assign rights and duties to the different bodies which would create the new infrastructure. Most urban areas received elected local authorities in 1835 but the creation of separate authorities for different purposes continued. In London the situation was particularly chaotic; the creation of the Metropolitan Board of Works in 1855 was the culmination of years of negotiation, between Poor Law unions, parishes, turnpike trusts, quarter sessions, and various improvement commissioners, with the City of London in particular fighting to maintain its independence and special powers. Even so, London still presented, as Best puts it: '. . . the anomalous spectacle of a great capital city without a unitary government; a natural whole, allowed to remain in a condition of separate parts.'[22] It was not until 1888 that London achieved that unitary government, only to have it removed once again by Margaret Thatcher in the 1980s.

In other parts of the country, matters were relatively simple. But, even when issues of local government had been sorted out, there remained the mammoth task of providing clean water, taking away sewage, laying pipes for gas supplies, building rail- and tramways. All of these required constant extensions as the towns and cities expanded. The work was undertaken both by public bodies, concerned principally with matters affecting public health, and by private companies which flourished in the field of transport, power, and light, although the line was often blurred; many private companies required public sanction, in the form perhaps of a local Act of Parliament, and towards the end of the century many local authorities undertook what became known as 'municipal socialism' in promoting and running gas, electricity, and transport undertakings. Whoever took the initiative, the investment was substantial.

Even before 1830, for example, every town in Britain with a population greater than 50,000 had a gas company and most towns with over 10,000 were similarly equipped; normally the company first secured a contract from the local authority to supply street lighting and then offered the service to private houses. Gas lighting was extremely popular, despite its poor quality before the invention of the incandescent mantle in the 1890s, and was universal in middle-class homes; it was only with the introduction of the prepayment meter, in the 1890s, that it spread widely among the working classes, while gas cooking also only developed fully at that time.[23] By as early as 1846, nearly £12 million had been invested in gasworks and investment continued thereafter, with particular expansion between 1865 and 1885.[24]

Another form of infrastructure investment took place in the last quarter of the century, with the establishment of telephone companies in most towns and their linking into the national trunk network. The telephone was adopted very rapidly, no doubt because of its utility to business; the early exchanges were in the large business centres. One observer wrote in 1882 that 'In 1877, it was a scientific toy; it has now grown to be a practical instrument'[25], partly through experiments along the private line which linked the works in Norwich of J & J Colman, the mustard-makers, with their offices in London. Innovation was so rapid that it is unclear whether London, Glasgow, or Manchester had the first exchange, but many large towns had them by 1881; by 1892, there were exchanges in over 660 places. The creation of a national network followed rapidly; by the late 1880s takeovers had led to control by six companies, by the early 1890s one company was in control and in 1912 it was bought by the state to form a national service under the Royal Mail.[26]

Tramways were a particularly urban form of transport. Construction really began only with the Tramways Act of 1870 but over 2,700 miles were in use by 1914. For the first two decades, they were mainly powered by horses; steam traction followed and then electricity. Their use expanded very rapidly, with 151 million passenger journeys in 1879 and 3,426 million in 1913–14;

the latter figure was 74 times the population of the United Kingdom and twice the number of rail journeys in the same year. Most tramways were built by private companies, but local authorities were given the power to acquire them and by 1914 owned two-thirds of the network.[27]

Tramways were only one example of the increasing role which was played in the economy by the local authorities of towns and cities. By 1913, local authorities provided or sold police, housing, bus, and tram services, gas, electricity, schools, and colleges, hospitals, cemeteries, roads, water, and drainage. They employed the vast majority of the 320,000 public employees counted by the 1911 census. They were successful traders and thus reduced local taxes; in one sample of authorities, trading profits were sufficient to cover all the costs of public health and the police.[28] As a result of this expansion into many areas of society and economy, by 1913 their capital and recurrent spending had become very substantial. Even in 1856, when records begin, municipal capital formation, partly for the construction of increasingly splendid municipal buildings, was nearly 10 per cent of total capital formation; the proportion increased during the rest of the century and was always much higher than capital spending by central government. At its maximum of £41 million in 1902, local government capital formation accounted for over 25 per cent of capital spending of all kinds in the United Kingdom.

Capital spending could be covered by the raising of loans, but the servicing of those loans together with normal recurrent spending by local authorities from local taxation—the rates—contributed to a crisis in local taxation in the Edwardian period to which neither the Conservative nor the Liberal party had an effective solution.[29] Part of the difficulty was the large relative size of local property taxes; in 1913 they raised £83 million at a time when central government raised £137 million from income and expenditure taxes. The effect was to increase the relative burden on property-owners.

Local authorities were important, however, in another way; they provided a counterweight to central government, emphasizing local needs and economic priorities. In the middle of the century, this role was more important than that of local welfare, which public opinion then felt was best left to charitable initiative. Later, however, Birmingham under Joseph Chamberlain in the 1870s gave a new slant to municipal enterprise by running local services and devoting the profits to town improvement, a lead followed by many local councillors who agreed with Chamberlain that the community should take a lead in dealing with social evils: 'Private charity is powerless, religious organisations can do nothing to remedy the evils which are so deep-seated in our system. . . . I venture to say that it is only the community acting as a whole that can possibly deal with evils so deep-seated.'[30] Chamberlain, too, set an example to others in his planning of Birmingham's city centre, working with private enterprise to tear down slums, to drive new and broader streets, and to erect grand offices and shops which replaced the crowded mess of workshops and houses which had hitherto characterized the centres of towns. This was not an unmixed blessing, in that such municipal enterprise often destroyed working-class housing, but it transformed the appearance of the nineteenth-century city.

Human capital formation

Much more difficult to measure than the physical growth of the cities was the simultaneous investment in the skills of the people who lived within them. Economists regard expenditure on education, training, health, and migration as a form of investment in 'human capital', by analogy with investment in physical capital formation, such as buildings and machinery; equipping a worker with a new machine will increase his or her productivity but so will teaching a new skill. Like physical capital formation, human capital formation involves actions by a number of investors, both public and private.

There was certainly enormous change. In 1830 schooling at all levels was a matter of voluntary initiative and there was no co-ordination between different educational institutions; 'By 1914

England, Wales and Scotland had something which could be called an educational system; and all members of the society were expected to have some encounter with formal schooling.'[31] The system, such as it was, was essentially created in the fifty years after the Education Act of 1870, which brought to an end decades of feuding between religious denominations over control of state funding of education, feuding which had been so intense that it had largely prevented state funding. By 1914, however, the working classes had been provided with a system of elementary education, which ended with entry into the job market at the age of 12 or 13. The middle classes had secondary education, sometimes leading to the newer urban universities, and the wealthy and the upper classes had the so-called public schools which offered entry into the older universities. Although exceptional individuals were able to jump the hurdles between the different sub-systems, they remained largely distinct, with different purposes, different funding, and different syllabuses.

It is important not to overestimate the importance of the creation of this system. First, Britain was already an increasingly literate nation before the 1870 Act could have had any influence, particularly since compulsory education did not come until 1880. Even in 1840, nearly 70 per cent of men and 50 per cent of women were already able to sign their name in the register when they got married; although this is a minimal test of writing skills, it is indicative of reasonable levels of reading skills in an age when reading was universally taught before writing. Just before the reforms of 1870 could have had any effect, the level of achievement was still higher, with about 85 per cent of each sex able to sign. Sunday schools and the so-called 'dame' or 'private adventure' schools which catered to the working classes had not done so bad a job with the basic skills of reading and writing.

It is much more difficult to estimate the extent to which the population possessed in 1830 or 1850, or came to possess later in the century, higher level skills including those of numeracy as well as literacy. The level of book and newspaper reading suggests that skills were not only acquired at school but continued to be practised with enjoyment; newspapers proliferated in late Victorian Britain, with 1,260 in existence in 1886 and 2,902 in 1900.[32] Book publishers produced large editions of popular fiction. Municipal and commercial lending libraries grew; by 1902 there were 900,000 volumes in London's public libraries. On the assumption that books and newspapers were not only read but also understood, readers were able to cope with quite sophisticated vocabularies and with an increasing use of number. There are other signs of numerical fluency. Street betting, though illegal, flourished, and the ability to bet implies a sophisticated ability to calculate probabilities, even if betting men did not see themselves as mathematical wizards. Systems to determine wages, based on piecework or on complex divisions between groups of workers, required an ability to calculate.

Acquiring the 'three Rs'—of reading, writing, and arithmetic—was a matter of joint investment between, increasingly, the state and the parents of the children being educated. At least in the early stages of compulsory education, the investment by the parents or by the children themselves was a less than willing one; mothers, who often relied on the labour of children to diversify and supplement the family income, were loath to dispense with it. School attendance was often intermittent and truancy a problem. Few working-class children were able to stay at school beyond the minimum leaving age, which was established at 10 in 1880 and rose to 12 by 1899.

Formal education increasingly came to be regarded as the business of society as well as of the individual. Much more problematical, and therefore the subject of hot debate and vicissitudes of policy throughout the late nineteenth century, was vocational training. Until the middle of the century, such training was seen as the joint responsibility of employer and worker or trainee; the ancient method of carrying it out, which still survived in many trades, was apprenticeship. The boy, and it was invariably a boy who was apprenticed, bound himself to a master for a term of years; the master undertook to teach the craft, the apprentice to learn, to follow the master's orders and to work for only a small wage or merely board and lodging. Apprenticeship could teach handicraft skills of the highest level; an engineering apprentice, for example, had to be able by the end of his training to produce a smooth surface in metal with the aid only of a hand file. Such skills continued to be needed in craft industries and for the increasing number employed in the repair of goods. There were still about 340,000 apprentices in Britain in the early years of the twentieth century, although apprenticeship was then becoming less appropriate as a method of training in many factory industries.[33] It survived in some industries only as a bargaining counter between employer, seeking to employ unskilled workers, and trade union seeking to protect the position of the skilled artisan. Where it did transfer from the traditional sectors such as paper-making or boot and shoe production to new technologies, it was often in a new form, with the journeyman taking over the teaching role and the master/employer no longer involved.[34]

In part, apprenticeship declined because it was an inappropriate method for learning the new technical skills which characterized modern industries; imitation was not an adequate basis for training in the chemical or electrical industries, where some scientific knowledge was needed for the bulk of the labour force. In the late nineteenth century there was great debate about the responsibility for providing that knowledge and the training needed to apply it to industry. Employers urged the state to provide: government argued that it should not usurp the proper role of employers. By the end of the century an uneasy truce had been reached, whereby the state provided, partly at school and partly through evening classes, for men and women to learn the scientific basis of their trade, while the employer and the workmen or women were expected to provide for the learning of the technical skills themselves.

The relatively slow development in Britain of formal education, at least as compared with several other European countries, and the truce over scientific and technical instruction, produced what was one of the great success stories of British society in the late nineteenth century: the evening class move-ment which was regarded with envy by the rest of the world. It began with the Mechanics' Institutes, formed in mid-century to give instruction to deserving artisans, both in cultural subjects, such as literature and art, and in vocational subjects, such as book-keeping and draughtsmanship. Evening classes were quickly established in all urban areas, relying both on public benevolence to provide the funding and on enthusiasm for learning and the acquisition of skills to provide the students. State funding followed, based at one stage on a levy on whisky, allowing a great expansion in classes. In that movement lies the history not only of adult education in Britain but also the origin of such institutions of higher education as Birkbeck College in the University of London or London Guildhall University, in which this book was written. The latter was founded in 1848 by the Bishop of London as the Metropolitan Evening Classes for Young Men.

Investment in education, both at school and through evening classes, was thus a substantial activity. In terms of results, there was undoubtedly an improvement in the quality of the labour force. It has been estimated that males born in England and Wales between 1836 and 1845 spent 4.7 years on average in formal schooling, while those born between 1907 and 1916 had 9.4 years, exactly double.[35] Technical training, largely part-time and undertaken after leaving school, was in addition to this; by 1897, nearly a quarter of a million students were taking examina-tions in craft and technical subjects of the City and Guilds of London Institute. As a result, in the 1911 census just over 30 per cent of the work-force was described as skilled manual workers; this ratio declined after 1911. A very rough estimate of the effects of both formal schooling and technical training is that the quality of labour improved by 0.3 per cent per annum from 1856–1873 and by 0.5 per cent from 1873–1913.[36] Though seem-ingly small, this was actually a substantial contribution both to the economic growth of the period and, since schooling and technical training improves lifetime earnings, to the welfare of the children and young people concerned.

Households in Victorian and Edwardian Britain thus invested in their own housing, in the development of the towns and cities around those houses, and in themselves. To create this material and human wealth, they went to work. So, it is to their working lives that we now turn.

5

CHANGING WORKPLACES

Work style

This and the previous chapter make a clear distinction between home and work. Such a distinction would have had little meaning for men and women living in the early nineteenth century, for it was then still normal for home to be workplace and for the family to work alongside man and wife. Only in a few occupations which had adopted the factory system was workplace physically separated from home, then often only by a few yards, and even in factories it was still commonplace for family members to work together. The restrictions which were imposed in the 1830s and 1840s on the labour of women and children in factories and mines, usually regarded as a triumph of philanthropic endeavour, were in fact often resisted by workers in those industries because they would separate family members.[1]

By 1914, however, the separation for male workers between home and work, which we now regard as normal, was largely complete. Paid work at home continued, but it was restricted either to men in craft and professional occupations or to women, required to work for long hours for a pittance and without any of the formal protections secured by the majority of workers. For most men, paid work meant 'going to work', for increasingly long distances as the commuter networks spread around the big cities. The middle classes were the first to move, followed by skilled artisans and then by the bulk of the working class. Commuting meant also a likely separation of workmates from friends, except perhaps for a pub visit at the end of the working day.

Women experienced an equally profound change. The sexual division of labour, which had always existed in the shape of men's and women's jobs in agriculture or craft occupations, was accentuated by the preponderance of work outside the household and by the increasing view that it was not respectable for a married woman to go out to work. In 1851, only a quarter of married women were not engaged in some form of employment; by 1911, only 10 per cent were employed. As male wages rose and home employment collapsed, working-class women redefined their roles, concentrating on housework and the care of children; homemaking skills, imparted increasingly through domestic economy teaching in schools, became celebrated in their own right. Many women resented the loss of independence and a wage; others saw in it a vindication of their separate role and status.[2]

The effects of these changes were very great. The establishment of factory, office, and shop as separate entities, with workers who were not family members, relatives, or even neighbours, implied discipline in timekeeping and attendance at work which had been absent from earlier generations. Custom, in the shape of taking days off to go to fairs or festivals or the so-called 'St Monday'—the habit for many workers of working on Saturdays but taking Monday off—was replaced by a fixed working week, fixed hours, and a rigorous enforcement of those hours. Artificial lighting allowed longer hours; in the eighteenth century the length of the working day had been regulated by the hours of daylight and therefore varied from summer to winter.

The length of the working week probably rose in the early nineteenth century, at least for factory workers; textile workers were expected to work from 6 a.m. to 7 or 8 p.m., with only an hour for meals. But the norm for most manual workers in the eighteenth century had been ten hours—a working day from 6 a.m. to 6 p.m. with two hours for meals—and this was reinstituted, at least for some factory workers, by the Ten Hours Act of 1847. Thereafter, a move to a nine-hour day occurred in most industries in the 1870s; a decrease in the working week, by treating Saturdays as 'half-holidays', came between the 1870s and the 1890s. Holidays tended to be centred on individual days at Christmas, Easter, and Whitsun, with some regional variations such as the 'wakes weeks' and Lancashire mill closures, and were given legislative support in the Bank Holidays Acts of 1871 and 1875, but paid holidays for extended periods of a week or more came only in the 1890s and thereafter, and then mainly for the skilled workers. Non-manual workers, with the notable exception of shop workers, normally worked shorter hours.[3]

An overall measure of these changes is that in 1856, average hours worked per year were 3,185, or 49 weeks of 65 hours; by 1913 this had fallen, to 2,744 hours composed of 48.8 weeks of 56.4 hours. Almost all the change, a fall of nearly 15 per cent, occurred in the 1870s. But, as hours fell, efficiency and intensity of work increased so that more was actually produced in a smaller number of hours.[4] In addition, commuting imposed an additional burden and an additional time away from home and family; a detailed study of the workforce of a London tailoring firm found, for example, that the average distance to work more than doubled, from 2.2 km. (1.4 miles) in the 1860s and 1870s to over 4.5 km. (2.8 miles) in the 1890s.[5] Among the middle classes of Newcastle upon Tyne, only 40 per cent lived at their workplace as early as 1840, but the average journey to work was only just over 0.8 km. (0.5 miles) and most still lived within the central urban area. By 1870 the average journey to work had doubled, with the professional classes moving furthest. By 1913 'a large proportion of the professional group lived outside the city altogether' and the average middle-class journey was 4.8 km. (3 miles).[6] Part of the reason for increased journey times was, of course, that transport links improved so as to make such journeys practicable. To some extent, therefore, the reduction in hours at work was offset by longer travelling times.

The location of work thus changed fundamentally. It is much more difficult to describe, except in great detail, the many alterations which took place in the content of jobs, what they consisted of, how they were done, what skills they required. Equally variable were conditions of work, the standards of heating, lighting, and general comfort in offices, shops, or factories. Moreover, the period from 1830 to 1914 was one in which not only did many jobs either appear or disappear as a result of changing tastes or changing technologies, but the whole shape of the workforce and its distribution across the country altered radically.

The distribution of work

Between 1841 and 1911, the proportion of the population engaged in agriculture fell, while the proportion in service occupations rose. That is the simplest way of describing the main change which occurred in what is known as 'the industrial distribution of the labour force', but like most simple statements it is deceptive not only in what it says but in what it leaves out. The complete picture is shown in Figures 5.1 and 5.2.

First, there was agriculture (including fisheries), which had been Britain's primary activity in the eighteenth century. It was already reduced to 22 per cent of the labour force by 1841 but fell further, in the most rapid change experienced by any sector, to 9 per cent by 1911. This marked Britain out from the rest of the world, because by the time of the First World War a third or more of the people in all other countries were still engaged in agriculture.

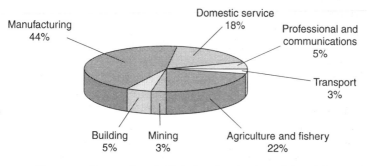

FIG. 5.1   Occupations in Britain, 1841 (male and female)

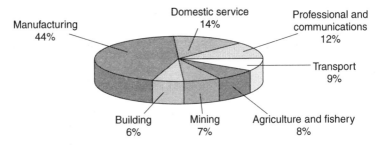

FIG. 5.2   Occupations in Britain, 1911 (male and female)

Second, the simple statement does not mention manufacturing. The making of things—including buildings—was already, by 1841, the occupation of nearly half the British labour force but the oddity, at least to anyone who mistakenly equates economic growth with manufacturing, is that this proportion rose only slightly, to exactly half, by 1911. If building and construction workers are excluded, then the proportion of workers in manufacturing works out at 43 per cent in 1841 and 44 per cent in 1911. Whatever the exact proportion, it was much higher in Britain, both in 1841 and in 1911, than in any other country in the world. This, and the continuing importance of manufacturing, was the legacy of its rise in the classical period of the Industrial Revolution.

Third, the simple statement omits mining. The extractive industries, wresting stone, coal, iron, and other metals from the ground, more than doubled in importance, from 3 per cent in 1841 to 7 per cent in 1911.

Fourth, and this was perhaps in the long run the most significant of ways in which Britain differed from the rest of the world, the service occupations—jobs which range from nurse to Governor of the Bank of England, from doctor to road sweeper, from shop assistant to coast guard—began the rise which, in the twentieth century, has made them Britain's pre-eminent activity. At the same time, their nature began to change. In 1841, 18 per cent of the labour force were engaged in personal and domestic service; 3 per cent in transport and communications; and 5 per cent in professional occupations, the civil and military services, and finance and commerce, a total of 26 per cent. By 1911, despite the conspicuous display of servants by the Edwardian upper and middle classes, the domestic and personal services had fallen to 14 per cent but, to counterbalance this, transport and communications had risen to 9 per cent and the other services to 12 per cent of the labour force, making a total of 35 per cent. The change in proportions was particularly marked among women, as Figures 5.3 and 5.4 show; in 1841 domestic and personal service was the occupation of 54 per cent of women in the paid workforce but this had fallen (although the actual number of women in such jobs increased) to 40 per cent in 1911 as other job and career opportunities widened.

Last, the simple statement is one about proportions, which is correct in examining the distribution of industry and of types of work. But, because the population rose so much between 1830 and 1914, the actual numbers of people working in a particular activity could rise even if the proportion fell. This was the case, for example, with agriculture; despite the rapid fall in the proportion of the population engaged in agriculture, there were actually slightly more people employed there in 1911 than in 1841 (though many fewer than in 1851): they were, however, doing very different things, as Chapter 6 will show.

These figures, dry as they may seem, both describe and prefigure changes which have fundamentally altered the economy of

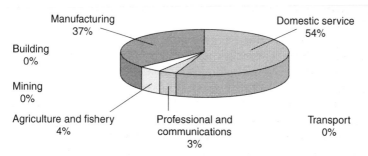

FIG. 5.3 Female occupations in Britain, 1841

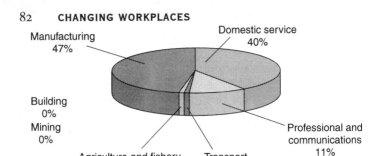

FIG. 5.4   Female occupations in Britain, 1911

Britain and the lives of its workers. They were the beginnings of the process which by the end of the twentieth century has made Britain into essentially a post-industrial nation, with only one-third or less of its labour force engaged in manufacture but nearly two-thirds in services or transport, while both agriculture and mining have been reduced to close to zero.

During this process the geographical distribution of work changed also, though not as much as the industrial distribution. A tension always exists between processing or manufacture close to where the raw materials are produced, be it farm, mine, or port, and processing or manufacture close to the market. In the eighteenth century, with markets highly dispersed both across the countryside at home and in many countries overseas, it made sense to locate production close to the source of raw materials or power; wrought or cast iron was produced close to the iron and coal mines, cotton goods in Lancashire where water power was available and raw cotton could be imported through Liverpool.

During the nineteenth century, the improvement of transport and the development of power which could be applied in many locations was combined with the increasing concentration of the market for goods in the big cities to free industry and manufac-turing to locate itself in new areas. The process was a slow one, partly because it did not make sense in many circumstances to move large numbers of workers and the factories and machines which they operated, just for the sake of reducing the costs of transport of finished goods. But, at the margin and over the decades, change occurred; in particular, London and the South-East, the location in particular of the service industries, gained at the expense of the traditional manufacturing areas in the North-east and North-west, a change which accelerated after the First World War.

This illustrates an important, even a vital, point about the changing nature of work. It is rarely dramatic, rarely sudden; rather it proceeds by the slow accretion of a myriad of individual decisions, each of which may be finely balanced, each of which seeks just a small advantage, a slightly greater profit, or a slightly smaller loss. It is natural to seek for heroic figures, entrepreneurs, or inventors who succeeded in economic life just as politicians or generals won wars, but most of the people who make decisions—either in the economy or in wars—are not heroic and the overwhelming number of decisions are small and piecemeal and yet ultimately together change the world.

Such changes affected each and every working person in Britain between 1830 and 1914 and form the subject of the next three chapters. But there were also some pervasive national or global changes, affecting all economic life and all working lives, which need first to be considered. The foremost were the use of interchangeable parts, changing technologies of communication, the internationalization of production and markets, and the growth of trade unionism.

Interchangeable parts

Before the nineteenth century, and to a large extent before 1850, each piece of equipment and each piece of manufactured output was made individually. This is not to say that goods were not made in large quantities; a popular or useful design would be copied many times over and, as Adam Smith pointed out in his famous description of a pin factory at the end of the eighteenth century, it was possible to take advantage of economies of mass production and specialization: one worker made the pin, another added the head, another sharpened the point. But such goods did not need to be exact copies of each other.

Nor, by and large, did such goods need to fit together with any exactitude. Bricks or tiles needed to be of approximately the same size and shape, bullets needed to have approximately the same diameter as the barrel of the musket, cotton or woollen cloth needed to be of approximately the same size and pattern. But approximation was enough. Only in a very few instances did it matter if one piece fitted exactly with another and, if it was necessary, then an exact fit was achieved by individual manufacture or adjustment of the fitting pieces. Thus a wheelwright would shape a wheel and axle to match each other, or the maker of a steam engine would manufacture the cylinder head to match the bore of the cylinder. This was not merely a matter of initial manufacture, but also of repair; when one component wore out, another had to be made individually to replace it.

The revolutionary change, achieved mainly in the second half of the nineteenth century and led by engineers in Britain and the United States, was to marry mass production together with parts which were replicated to fine tolerances and were thus interchangeable. It was this revolution which made possible mass production in the sense in which the twentieth century knows it, where one axle for a particular model of car is exactly like another. Even more fundamentally, and this is where interchangeability really began with the work of a British engineer, Joseph Whitworth, one screw or bolt is exactly like another.

Interchangeable parts depended on exact measurement and thus on a range of measuring tools such as micrometers. But they depended even more on the ability of machines and tools to be set to operate at levels of accuracy which were greater than could ever be achieved by hand and to do this in the working of metals which were too hard to be shaped by hand tools. In the 1830s, British engineers in a very few workshops could use steam hammers to beat metal castings into rough shape; they could use planing machines to produce an approximately flat surface, and they could use lathes and boring machines to produce curves. But all depended on finishing by hand with a file and thus the products could not be truly interchangeable.

By 1914, by contrast, interchangeable metal parts of great accuracy and complexity could be produced by a whole range of machine tools; moreover, the principles of interchangeability, developed in metal- and wood-working, had been applied throughout manufacturing. Boots and shoes were now made up of parts precisely cut and shaped by machinery, clothes were tailored from parts cut exactly to size, while all forms of producer and consumer durables, from ploughs to rifles, from bicycles to electric light bulbs, could be bought in the knowledge that they would fit together and that, if they should break or need repair, a spare part could easily be bought.

The repercussions on working life, as on domestic life, were dramatic. Hand skills were devalued; they did not become worthless, since there continued to be a demand for individual production particularly of luxury goods and for the repair and maintenance of machine-made goods. But by contrast, new skills were required, of setting and operating machines, which required an acquaintance with measuring equipment and the ability to read and interpret complex designs and patterns. Those patterns and designs could themselves be replicated, using the new technology of 'blueprints' and distributed worldwide if need be, so that parts could be made separately from the finished product. Interchangeability had made possible a machine civilization in Britain and its diffusion throughout the world.

Communications

The revolution in communications between 1830 and 1914 was equally momentous in its impact on working lives but, while interchangeable parts had their greatest effect on manufacturing, the technology of communications transformed commerce. Paradoxically, it was probably not so much the dramatic inventions such as the railway which had the greatest economic effect but the less obvious, the improved postal services, the telegraph and the telephone, buses and trams.

The paradox stems from the fact that the aspect of the railway which most impressed onlookers, then and since its introduction into Britain for the carriage of people in 1830, was its speed, which benefited passengers but was of little use to most forms of goods traffic. It matters little to the purchaser of a ton of coal whether the sacks have taken three weeks, three days, or three hours to get from pit to factory or domestic hearth, provided that the coal is there when it is needed; in other words, it is regularity of supply, not speed, which is important. A secure supply may indeed incur costs, since the coal merchant may have to keep slightly higher stocks or inventories, but the dangers of significant interruptions to supply were not very great even before the building of the canals and insignificant thereafter; unlike North America, Britain did not suffer every winter from the freezing of rivers and canals.

Where the railway did have an advantage over earlier forms of transport was in carrying perishable goods. But, once again, this can be overestimated. The railway aided agricultural specialization and made it possible to grow crops on the soils which suited them best; it allowed early crops of vegetables and flowers, grown in the West of England, to reach London markets. But the impact on most consumers, or even on most farmers, was small. Market gardening and dairying for all but the most luxury trade continued to cluster around the large towns. The traditional method of moving livestock, driving it on the hoof to the cities, did gradually disappear, no doubt to the benefit of the cows, sheep, pigs, and poultry involved, but still remained common throughout the century.

The railway did play its part, but very much in partnership with other forms of transport such as buses and trams, in making possible the separation of home from work which notably occurred between 1830 and 1914. The development of Victorian housing, for all classes of society, depended on cheap, rapid, and reliable transport which could not ultimately be provided, at least for the volume of passengers which came to be required, by horse-drawn cabs or stagecoaches, or later by horse trams and horse-buses. This was in part because of the sheer number of horses that were, or would have been, needed; because a horse bus, carrying twenty-five or more people, was so heavy that its two horses needed to be changed frequently, each bus required ten or more horses. Their impact on urban life in terms of their need for food and their dung were considerable; by the end of the century about 1 million tons of horse droppings had to be removed each year from London's streets. The number of journeys in London increased, nevertheless, from 60 million in 1860 to 300 million in 1896, although provincial cities were much less well served. In such cities and outside the centre of London, however, the horse tram became important and traffic continued to grow throughout the century.

The growth in both passenger and goods traffic, largely horse-drawn, created massive traffic jams in many cities. By contrast, railways were initially enormously disruptive as they were driven through built-up areas but thereafter helped to remove traffic from the roads. They were also, in a psychological sense, liberating to large sections of the community. They adapted themselves with ease to the Victorian class system; commuters were not only segregated into first-, second- and third-class carriages but, by the device of 'workmen's fares' for early morning travel and reduced fares for clerks, into groups which arrived one after the other, but not together, at the London termini.[7] Trams and buses played a part in altering the industrial structures of many towns and in contributing towards the segregation of classes at home which was reinforced by the split between residence and place of work. By and large, it was the upper and middle classes who took earliest and greatest advantage of transport improvements, which allowed them to escape from urban contamination, both physical and moral, into the suburbs which grew up around London and all the major urban areas.

Work itself, however, was greatly affected by improvements to the postal system and the invention and rapid spread of telegraph and telephone. Between 1840 and 1889 the number of letters delivered rose from 169 million to 1,558 million.[8] Post offices multiplied—515 opened in 1854 alone—and by the end of the century London had twelve and Birmingham six deliveries each day.[9] But urgent orders could be placed at once by telegraph or, later by telephone, for delivery by rail or by the parcel post which was established in 1883.[10] The first Electric Telegraph Company was established in 1846, although the invention itself was several decades older. Growth thereafter was very rapid, with 99,216 messages transmitted in 1851 and 745,880 in 1855. The age of immediacy had arrived.

As with the impact of railways, the economic impact of communications technology is more complex than it seems at first sight. In practice, a London tailor in the 1830s wanting cloth would probably not send an order direct to a Manchester mill, but instead would send a messenger to a London wholesaler who kept stocks of cloth which, experience had taught, London tailors were likely to need. Keeping such stocks in London had a cost—economists speak of the opportunity cost of holding and warehousing the stocks or alternatively of the interest which could be gained if that money had been invested—but it was probably not very much more than the costs of keeping the same stocks in Manchester, waiting there for an order. However, even small savings are worth having and new communications made them possible.

Probably more important was the improvement in market information. Modern economic theory normally assumes that economic agents—entrepreneurs, manufacturers, shoppers—possess perfect information; they know the price of the goods which they need and whether and where they are available. In practice, such knowledge is imperfect even today, despite Yellow Pages and similar sources of information, but it was much more so in the nineteenth century. This gave rise to significant risks. Even after the advent of steam shipping, a merchant trading with North America in the 1840s might have to make decisions about the goods to send on a ship some three weeks before the ship could arrive in New York or Charleston, on the basis of information which had left America at least another three weeks before, and in ignorance of what other merchants were loading on their ships; the ship's captain or factor would have to buy raw cotton for the return journey without knowing the state of demand for cotton in Lancashire. The situation was even worse in other markets; a voyage under sail from Britain to Australia could take eight months, but even a steamship from London to Sydney took 134 days in 1839, 119 days in 1849.

With the coming of the telegraph such information came easily to hand, even if the physical transport of the goods was still slow and cumbersome. The world was still a long way from the global market place of the late twentieth century, with instantaneous communication and dealing, computer to computer, around the world, but major steps had been taken in the reduction of risk.

The internationalization of economic life

Communications were but one aspect of a growing internationalization of economic life, in which Britain led the way and which affected everyone as worker or consumer. Britain was, of course, already accustomed to trade with the rest of the world. In 1855, approximately 23 per cent of the goods (including food) consumed in Britain were imported and 15 per cent of goods made in Britain were exported. In addition, Britain had the largest fleet of merchant ships, many of them used for trade far from home; it was already acting as banker and insurer to the trade of many other countries.

What occurred after 1830 was, therefore, a change of scale rather than of nature, but it was a very substantial one. In 1913, despite growing competition from such countries as France, Germany, and the United States, Britain was the world's largest investor, owning assets abroad greater than those three countries combined; it owned most of the world's shipping, financed most of the world's trade, made and exported over 25 per cent of the world's trade in manufactured goods and headed the largest empire and commonwealth which the world had ever known. In 1913 Britain was exporting 25 per cent of its output at the same time as the largest economy in the world, the United States, exported only 7 per cent.

The impact of international trade varied, of course, from one part of the economy to another. At one extreme, there were cotton goods, where all the raw material was imported and a very high proportion of the cotton thread and cloth was exported. At the other, there were industries, such as the supply of liquid milk, or some of the services, which were, in the jargon of economists, non-traded, impervious to foreign competition. But no one in Britain, unlike many other countries, was untouched by the international economy.

Foreign migration alone saw to that. Of the millions who left, perhaps half returned after a short or long period, bringing with them an experience of life overseas. But the majority stayed and settled, writing home, encouraging others to follow, buying familiar British goods, seizing opportunities to export goods which they hoped might appeal to the British market, borrowing money from Britain to finance ports, railways, plantations, and factories. Their letters, postcards, and parcels ensured that Britons felt part of the wider world.

Even for those who stayed at home, the impact of overseas trade, in both goods and services, was immense. The sheer range of raw materials, foods, and manufactured goods which became available itself improved British living standards, for increasing variety is an important component of consumption and economic welfare. At the same time, as a result of improved transport and of investment overseas in developing new sources of supply, there was a decline, persisting through most of the late nineteenth century, in the prices of imported goods, from bananas to Chinese silks, from New Zealand lamb to the teak furniture which graced many Victorian parlours.

It became fashionable in the 1870s and 1880s, at the first statement of a theme which has been played and replayed ever since, to express concern about the volume of imports, particularly those which seemed directly to compete with goods made in Britain. Whatever the impact on individual industries, and there were certainly some which suffered greatly, the central fact

is that between 1830 and 1914, Britain earned far more by foreign trade—both in goods and in services such as banking and
insurance—than it spent, leaving growing trade surpluses to be
invested in assets overseas which themselves later brought investment income back to Britain. Trade gave employment to
British workers, better, cheaper, and more varied goods to British consumers, markets for British entrepreneurs, and 'un-
earned' income to British investors. The British economy could
have grown without this trade, as other economies did, but it
would have been a very different economy from that which
entered the twentieth century.

Trade unions

Early in the nineteenth century, any attempt by a group of
workers to band together to secure improvements in their
wages or working conditions was illegal, outlawed by the
Combination Acts which had been rushed through Parliament in 1799 and 1800 in fear of contagion spreading across the
English Channel from the French Revolution. By 1880, there
were about 500,000 members of trade unions while, by the time
of the First World War, they had, collectively, 4,145,000 members, had been given special legal privileges by legislation and
took part in negotiations with employers both locally and na-
tionally.[11] About half of all adult manual workers were then
members.[12]

This transformation in working practices and in the status of
both worker and employer was not easily achieved, even though
the Combination Acts were never wholly effective. Initial attempts to organize trade unions, even after the repeal of the
Acts in 1824 and 1825, were met with fierce resistance by employers, by judges, and by government. The Tolpuddle Martyrs,
six men transported to Australia in 1834 for attempting to organize a trade union for agricultural labourers, were a symbol of
early trade unionism, and many who tried to emulate them were
dismissed or victimized in various ways; strikes and pickets remained illegal for many years, considered by the legal system to

be 'in restraint of trade', and employers often responded to them by lockouts.

Unlike the Tolpuddle Martyrs, most early trade unionists were drawn from the skilled trades, where the unions could rely for their subscriptions on relatively well-paid workers and where members could be offered benefits, such as support in seeking work and minimal payments at times of sickness. Such unions had many of the attributes, and the attraction to potential members, of friendly societies, but the majority attracted only small memberships and did not often come into conflict with employers. It was only in the 1850s, with the advent of the so-called 'new model' unions, aiming to recruit the bulk of workers in a particular industry, that a mass trade union movement grew, leading to the foundation in 1868 of the Trades Union Congress as the national voice of organized labour. By 1900 the political power of the organized working class was recognized both in the foundation of the Labour Party as the voice of the trade union movement and by the recognition of that political power in the legislative reforms of the Liberal government in 1907, which gave legal sanction to trade union activity and legal protection to the funds of the unions.

The strength of trade unionism remained based, at least until the twentieth century, in the skilled occupations; partly as a result, union power and influence were much greater in some parts of the country than in others. Lancashire, Yorkshire, and other parts of the North of England were particularly strong recruiting grounds, while rural areas remained infertile soil. Engineers, printers, shipwrights, cotton workers, and miners were archetypal union members. Some unions resisted technical change or became guardians of restrictive practices; their function was, after all, to protect the scarcity value of skilled labour and to do so by regulating the supply of labour.[13] But the reforms which trade unions (or alternatively the threat or promise of the political power of organized labour), brought about at the end of the nineteenth and the beginning of the twentieth centuries benefited all working people. Some protection for groups of workers, in particular women and children, who were thought incapable of driving a fair bargain with an employer or protecting themselves in other ways, had stemmed from the efforts of philanthropists, such as Lord Shaftesbury, or utilitarian reformers, such as Edwin Chadwick. But later in the century, other measures, both those directly benefiting groups of workers, such as miners or seamen, and general laws to promote health and safety at work, were achieved by the trade unions.

More problematic is the impact that trade unions had on the wages of their members. While trade unionists have naturally argued that their efforts raised wages, economists have countered, first, that in theory and in free market conditions wages will follow productivity trends and, second, that in practice wages rose because of the prosperity of industries rather than because trade unions were successful in securing an increased share of the proceeds. It is extremely difficult to separate cause from effect; wages may rise because an industry is doing well, at the same time as workers join a trade union because they feel more secure. Overall, there was very little direct relationship in the long run during the late nineteenth century between the growth of numbers of trade unionists and growth in wages, although it is arguable that trade unionism made it more difficult for employers to cut wages in bad times.

But what makes trade unions important is the change which their growth signalled in the relationship between employer and worker. Whether for good or ill, and many mourned the passing of the close relationship between master and man which had characterized the old craft workshops, that relationship was changed by the factory, the large enterprise and the breakdown of old forms of apprenticeship and recruitment. The trade unions symbolize that change, together with the growing political power of the working class through the extension of the franchise. Their growth was thus among the most important of the changes which altered the nature of work in the nineteenth century.

6

FOOD AND AGRICULTURE

Adaptation and adaptability

Farmers are often thought of disparagingly, at least by town-dwellers, as being 'stuck in the mud', slow to change or adopt new crops, clinging to old ways. This fits with a strong tradition in English literature which emphasizes the timeless joys of the rural life. Elizabeth Gaskell's *North and South*, published in 1855, is only the most obvious example of the contrast which many writers observed between rural existence, with roses around the cottage door, and the dourness and grime of the factory town.

The concept of an unchanging countryside peopled by paternalistic squires and parsons, and by deferential yeomen and labourers, all clinging to old folk ways and defying the forces of economics, does not reflect reality at any time. Farmers, landowners, and farm labourers may be attached to rural life; they may derive from it what economists call 'psychic income', satisfactions which cannot be expressed in monetary terms, just as lawyers cling to their wigs and gowns, or businessmen to their chauffeur-driven cars. But countrymen and countrywomen are as astute as townsmen and townswomen; like everyone else, they need to make a living. Over the centuries, they have very greatly altered their ways of doing so.

So it was from 1830 to 1914. Between those years, British agriculture came to work within an entirely new economic environment and, to achieve this, British landowners, farmers and workers demonstrated great adaptability. Historians argue, of course, about whether they could have done more, or about whether agriculture altered more or less rapidly than the rest of the economy, but the extent of the change is not in dispute. Its major facets were the departure of large numbers from country-side to town or overseas, substantial change in the types of agriculture undertaken in the different regions of Britain and an improvement in farming methods and equipment which made farm workers much more productive than ever before.

British agriculture, to use those words as a shorthand for the lives and decisions of several million landowners, farmers and workers, had to cope after 1830 with a major change in its economic environment. Agriculture was nurtured by govern-ments during the Napoleonic Wars, when it was an overwhelm-ing priority to feed the nation; after the wars, although it would have been possible to resume the import of food which had been increasing in the eighteenth century, the power of the landed interest—landowners and farmers—was able to achieve a prohi-bition on the import of grain unless the price rose very high. As was mentioned in Chapter 1, the Corn Laws, as this form of protection of agriculture at the expense of purchasers of food was called, became in the 1830s and 1840s the focus of popular and political agitation in favour of free trade, which had been advocated in the late eighteenth century by Adam Smith at a time when trade was carefully regulated and British industries heavily protected.

Some rationalization of the complex system of tariffs (duties on imports) took place in the 1820s and 1830s, but the decisive step towards free trade in all but agriculture was taken by Sir Robert Peel in his budget of 1842, which introduced income tax—it was said merely as a temporary measure—in the place of the money which government had received from tariffs. Although there was some grumbling from industries whose protection from foreign competition was reduced or removed, the strength of British manufacturing was already such that no serious harm resulted. The main effect, therefore, was to lead the Anti-Corn Law League, a mainly middle-class movement devoted to promoting free trade, to redouble its efforts. The combination of its arguments, increasing economic prosperity after 1842 and, possibly, the Irish potato famine, so convinced Peel that he was prepared in 1846 to repeal the Corn Laws, despite the fact that it split his Conservative Party for many years.

Like most political movements, the Anti-Corn Law League was supported by different people for different motives. Most economists at the time advocated repeal on theoretical grounds and because it would bring cheaper food; to most campaigners the attraction lay in lower prices; to many industrialists the attraction lay in being able to pay lower wages if food became cheaper. But the fact that food, and particularly bread, would be cheaper if imports were freely allowed itself stemmed from the other major change in the economic environment for British agriculture, the development of new and cheaper sources of food overseas. It was because of these linked changes, not just because of repeal, that agriculture had to adapt after the 1840s. The ramifications were felt far beyond the grain growers and their landlords: by dairy farmers, market gardeners, seedsmen and nurserymen, flower farmers, butchers, black-smiths, wheelwrights, carters, and agricultural machinery makers.

This very incomplete list makes the point that agriculture, like any industry, is composed of many more people than those who actually till the soil. Farmers and farm workers are most visible, but behind them are those who supply them with the tools and equipment which they need and those, workers in what are now collectively called the 'food industries', who process the food and transport it, bulky and heavy as it is, to the consumer. During the nineteenth century, the balance between these three groups shifted decisively, as it has continued to do in the twentieth century; fewer people grew or bred their own food, while equipment became ever more sophisticated and so did process-ing methods. As a result, farmers and farm workers in 1914 and even more so today make up a very small fraction of those who produce and distribute food. That change is itself proof of the adaptability of agriculture.

More and better food

As incomes rose, consumers demanded both more and better food. In some cases, the main impact on the consumer was through price. Wheat, the main bread grain, was at first made artificially expensive by the Corn Laws, but even after repeal, the growth of demand meant that its price remained at much the same level; from the 1860s, however, increasing quantities of wheat were imported, initially from northern Europe but then increasingly from North America. In 1885, Britain produced 2,145,000 tons of wheat at home but imported 3,075,000 tons, together with a further 792,000 tons of meal and flour.[1] By that time, the United States and India had each surpassed Russia as a source of supply, with Germany, Canada, and Australia lagging behind. But few of those who ate the bread knew or cared; what mattered to them was that the price of a 4 lb. loaf, which had been 10.5 pence in 1830, was by 1885 down to 6.23 pence and that by 1913, when an even larger proportion of wheat and flour was imported, the price had fallen yet more to 5.8 pence.[2]

One measure suggests that the average fall in the prices of vegetable products was 35 per cent between 1830 and 1910, at a time when animal products actually rose in price by 9 per cent and industrial and agricultural prices fell by 11 per cent.[3] Moreover, these falling prices for fruit, vegetables, and grains do not take full account either of improvements in the quality of particular foods or of less tangible benefits of the ever-widening range of foods which came to be available in British shops. The quality of bread probably improved as a result of laws to prevent the adulteration of flour with substances such as chalk, so that the fall in the price of bread underestimates the benefit to those who ate it. More obvious a benefit were the imports of tropical foodstuffs—2,804,700 bunches of bananas were consumed in Britain in 1902—which became possible with the introduction of refrigerated ships from the 1880s, although most such foods remained out of the reach of all but the richer shoppers.

Prices of meat and dairy products did not change so markedly. In part, this was because some, liquid milk being the best example, were not subject to foreign competition. But rising wages and the declining prices for non-animal products, such as bread and potatoes, which tended to be the basic items in the diet, also made it possible for consumers to spend more on meat, milk, butter, and cheese, thus ensuring that demand grew more rapidly than did the population. Questions of taste also entered in; few were concerned whether the flour from which their bread was made came from Britain, Russia, or Australia, but imported meat, whether canned or frozen, was generally regarded as inferior to Scotch beef or Welsh lamb. Both demand for, and the prices of, home-produced meat held up well against foreign competition, although in other areas, such as bacon-curing and cheese-making, European producers swept the board.

Taken together, imports and home production gave an increasing choice of raw materials. This was supplemented by the development of a food processing industry, which even by the second quarter of the nineteenth century had largely supplanted home produce, despite William Cobbett's diatribe in 1821: 'How wasteful and indeed how shameful for a labourer's wife to go to the baker's shop.'[4] Butchers and bakers had always cooked and processed food, from black pudding, cooked ham, and sausages to cakes, biscuits, and muffins. But the late nineteenth century saw the development of large-scale, sometimes factory, production of such goods and their retailing and advertising on a national or sometimes international scale. Food processing and distribution was one of the main stimuli to the development of wholesaling and retailing, as we shall see in Chapter 9.

There were similar developments in drink where beer, the predominant alcoholic drink in England, was increasingly brewed by a declining number of large firms, supplying a national market over the railway network; by 1890, only 10 per cent of beer was brewed by retailers themselves.[5] The change coincided with a move away from porter to lighter pale ales and bitter. Concentration also occurred in the making of Scotland's national drink, whisky, with the growth in popularity of blended whiskies produced by a small number of firms in the Lowlands. Despite the increasing efforts of the temperance movement, whose most visible manifestation was the Salvation Army founded by William Booth in 1862, consumption of beer nearly doubled, reflecting the pub culture which increasingly became the archetypal leisure pursuit of much of the population, although consumption of home-produced spirits fell. In 1830, each person—man, woman or child—in Britain consumed on average 16.9 gallons of beer and 0.8 gallons of spirits, while by 1910 consumption had risen to 31.0 gallons of beer but fallen to 0.5 gallons of spirits. Meanwhile, imports of wine, largely for the upper classes—although port and lemon was said to be a favourite of working-class women—rose from £3.6 million in 1854 to £4.2 million in 1910.

While the pub flourished, the late nineteenth century also saw an increasing trend towards eating in restaurants and cafes or buying from street stalls and fish and chip shops. The combination of fish and chips, now regarded as the archetypal British dish, seems to have arisen simultaneously in London and in Lancashire. In London it sprang from the sale of fried fish among the Jewish community in Soho, chips being added in the 1850s or 1860s; in Lancashire, by contrast, the chips came first—often together with tripe or cow-heels. Fish and chips grew rapidly in popularity, particularly after the introduction of the steam trawler in the 1880s guaranteed a supply of cheap fish; thereafter, the retail trade was the basis of a large fishing fleet. It took 25 per cent of the catch by 1914 and up to 10 per cent of the potato crop. There were about 10,000–12,000 fish and chip shops in Britain in 1888, but 25,000 by 1910, by which time it is estimated that 'Many, perhaps most, working-class families in industrial areas used the fish and chip shop three or four times a week.' This was possible because of the density of shops; in 1911 there were 2,000 within a five-mile radius of Manchester Town Hall. Although it was cheap, convenient, and nutritious, fish and chips always had the odour of the slums; to the middle classes it had the attraction of forbidden fruit.[6]

There were other changes in the diet and habits of the nation. Chocolate ceased to be a drink of the leisured classes and became, whether on its own or in biscuits and cakes, a favourite food of the whole nation, if not of advocates of its dental health. However, the greatest growth was in tea, which sprang from relative obscurity at the beginning of the century to become the archetypal British drink, from afternoon tea in the palace to the solace of the housewife and the workman. What made this possible, above all, was purer water, one of the greatest achievements of the sanitary reformers, but the temperance movement and emulation of the upper classes did their bit. So did falling import duties and wider sources of imports, so that from the 1860s green China tea was replaced by black Indian, drunk with milk to the delight of the dairy industry. A whole new institution, the tea shop, grew up to cater for the new drink and Lyons or ABC became the resort of lovers and the respectable middle and working class.[7]

Better and more varied food, and more of it, was available for those who could pay. Food, like income and wealth, was unevenly distributed, particularly in an age when, in the Edwardian period, dining became a major means of the display of opulence and fat something to be prized rather than combated by dieting or healthy eating. The menus of Victorian and Edwardian banquets, with their many courses and increasingly elaborate and costly dishes, are ample testimony to this form of ostentation or conspicuous consumption, but even middle-class households schooled by the cookery books of Mrs Beeton appear to have consumed far more food than would be customary today.

But many could not afford even the nutritious broths which middle-class observers exhorted working-class mothers to feed to their children. Recall that, as Rowntree and other observers found even at the beginning of the twentieth century, up to one-third of the working class could not regularly afford enough food to maintain health and provide sufficient energy for work. Even so, the declining food prices of the latter part of the century, together with gradually increasing money wages, did make it possible for all but the very poor to buy more, to buy different foods and perhaps to have something more over for clothing, housing, and consumer goods.

Studies of food consumption thus show a gradual increase in

quantity, quality, and variety. Diets up to the 1860s contained substantial amounts of bread and potatoes, supplemented by an increasing consumption of sugar and, to a lesser extent, meat. From then, however, bread consumption fell and the use of potatoes stabilized as they were increasingly eaten with meat or fish rather than on their own; consumption per head of both meat and sugar is thought to have doubled between 1860 and 1914, as, in the urban areas, did the drinking or other use of milk, particularly to accompany porridge.[8]

The exact impact of these changes on the nutrition of the people is elusive, especially because so little is known about the distribution of food within the household; there is plenty of anecdotal evidence that the men got the lion's share, while women went short, but this is not easily translated into measurements of caloric intake. Studies of diet show improving intakes on average in the late nineteenth century; this was translated, at least from the 1860s onwards, into a gradual increase in the height of the population, but there remained many among the poor whose food intake must have been too little to sustain work and growth and at the same time to combat disease. Many children and adults were thus stunted and wasted—too short and too thin—and took in too little energy to let them work hard for a full day. For such people, the easier availability of tropical fruits such as bananas and oranges was of little significance; they just needed more food.

The agricultural response

Landlords, farmers and farm workers thus faced what must often have seemed a bewildering set of pressures and signs. Population growth, rising incomes, and the increasing size of towns meant greater overall demand. But imports and changing tastes made some old favourites among crops unprofitable. As a result, all three groups of people had to make apparently revolutionary changes in attitudes, products, and methods in order to survive.

The years between 1830 and 1860 saw the final part of the so-called Agricultural Revolution, a period when output rose to meet the challenge of a rising population. This was made possible by a series of linked innovations. Tenure patterns were altered, from those which had existed since the Middle Ages, by the concluding stages of the Enclosure movement; this was the name given to the process, which gained momentum in the eighteenth century, by which open fields, divided into strips, were replaced by enclosed farms. New crops such as the potato became common and old crops and animals were improved. In the last stages of the process, in the period known as that of 'High Farming', landlords and farmers invested heavily in improvements to buildings, to the land through drainage schemes and to livestock through scientific breeding. This investment was accompanied by the employment of more workers and output increased very greatly, although productivity did not change so rapidly.

High farming took place in an era of rising demand and rising or stable prices. Between 1860 and 1914, by contrast, the prices which British agriculture received for its output fell by nearly 20 per cent; the prices of some products, such as wheat, fell much more.[9] The fall was particularly fierce, at nearly 40 per cent, between 1862 and 1896, after which there was some recovery. These trends were partly the result of foreign competition under the new conditions of free trade, partly of technological change and increased efficiency. The individual British landowner, tenant farmer or farm worker, could do little or nothing to affect the trends; their job was to react to them.

Because their interest, and their power, was different, each of the three groups reacted differently. First, the landowners; 95 per cent of agricultural land was owned by landlords but farmed by tenant farmers. Such land was often the main, but not usually the only, source of income for the landlord; it was also for most landlords a source of prestige, pride, and status. This was so whether the landlord and his family came from the ancient aristocracy or squirearchy, or whether they had recently bought land with wealth earned in manufacture or commerce. Land established their place in society and often conferred political power. Landowners thus were content to receive a long-term return on their ownership and investment; they also derived so much status and satisfaction from their position that they would do almost anything to retain it.

Their reaction was, therefore, to attempt to use their political power to alleviate the situation, while trying to protect themselves from what they hoped would be a short-term decline in their rental incomes. Political attempts to restore tariff protection for food were, however, entirely unsuccessful, despite several Royal Commissions which documented agricultural distress; this failure, in sharp contrast to the success of various European aristocracies when faced with similar pressures, signalled the reduced political power of land compared to commerce and industry. Tenant farmers were, meanwhile, citing the decline in prices so as to exert pressure on their landlords to accept lower rents or to assist tenants in improvements which would enable them to grow new crops with a higher return. Landlords seem, despite their complaints, to have been largely able to resist these pressures until the 1890s; thereafter, however, their share of all income from agriculture fell sharply.

The second group, the tenant farmers, were less able to take a long view; they needed to earn an income year by year. Like landlords, they had much at stake; although most tenancies were formally only for the life of the tenant, many had inherited their farms from father and grandfather and had themselves invested in their equipment and buildings. During the Depression, many continued to invest in buildings, drainage, and fertilizers despite the apparent insecurity of their position. In addition to the need to earn a return on this investment, farmers like landlords derived status from their position and inheritance. But farmers had fewer resources and a greater need, therefore, rapidly to adapt to the new conditions or to face the loss of their farm and livelihood. Some could not cope and suffered such loss, for landlords did not find it difficult, despite the depressed conditions, to find tenants for vacant farms; but the majority sought new crops, new activities, to maintain or if possible to increase their incomes.

The evidence for this can be found in the changing use and

appearance of the British countryside. Rising grain prices in the first half of the nineteenth century had brought an increase in the area of tillage as opposed to grassland, but this movement was reversed as cheap imports bit into the market. Pastoral farming expanded in central and western England and to some extent in Scotland; the eastern areas with their drier soils, where the better growing conditions helped to increase average yields per acre, concentrated on grain. There was a further concentration within grain-growing areas, with wheat becoming concentrated on the heavier lands in the south-east, while oats and barley continued to be widely grown. Cropping was further diversified by the continued rise of root crops, both for animal and for human food, throughout the country.

The reduction in grain production was balanced by increases in livestock acreage, as Figure 6.1 shows.[10]

Sheep-farming was widely spread, since sheep could be combined with other uses of the land in many different cropping systems, although their numbers fell as farmers faced increased imports of mutton and wool. The keeping of cows was more

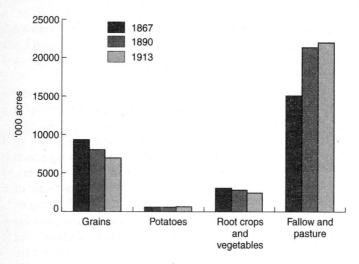

FIG. 6.1   The acreage of crops in Britain, 1867, 1890, and 1913

concentrated; the established dairying areas of north-west England and south-west Scotland were joined by a large area of southern England. From there the great urban areas could be supplied by railway with liquid milk, immune from foreign competition. Last, farmers diversified into woodland, which increased by about 27 per cent between 1873 and 1911, into fruit production in orchards, up by 21 per cent over the same period, and above all into market gardens, which grew in area by 145 per cent; in addition many arable farmers began to grow vegetables as field crops.[11]

Despite these responses, farmers as a group suffered badly between the 1860s and the 1890s, compared with both landlords and workers, although their position improved thereafter, as prices stabilized or improved, and the efficiency of farming increased. In part, the poor position of farmers until the 1890s stemmed from their changing power in relation to the third group involved in agriculture, farm workers. At the individual level, the farm labourer remained highly dependent on and subservient to his employer; customs such as yearly employment at hiring fairs, the poor education of most farm workers, and their isolation, all combined to restrict the power of the individual farm worker. Machinery was sometimes worked by contract labour, as in threshing. The labourer had little defence against a farmer who wanted to reduce his labour force by the use of machines.

But, at the same time, the economic situation at home and overseas made it increasingly possible for farm workers as a group, particularly the young men and women, to find alternative employment; there were jobs in the towns and more in North America or Australasia. Although farmers exaggerated the extent to which only boys and old men were left as labourers, the possibility of alternative jobs, and probably the work of agricultural trade unions, raised farm wages as the labour force shrank.[12] The farm labour force fell by 25 per cent between 1862 and 1896, although only by 1 per cent more between 1896 and 1910; agricultural wages, however, rose by 15 per cent before 1896 and by 20 per cent thereafter. As the labour force shrank and the education and skills of farm labourers improved, they became less dispensable, more a vital source of the increased efficiency on which farmers now depended.

It is always difficult, whether at the time or in retrospect, to know whether landlord, farmer, or labourer resisted change or welcomed it; no doubt some fought while others rejoiced or at least made the best of it. Some left the land bitter because they could no longer find a job, others welcomed the joys of life in the towns. It is, however, undeniable that British agriculture changed greatly between 1830 and 1914, reacting for the most part quickly, or at least as rapidly as the rest of the economy, to the new economic environment.

Methods of work

Farm labour is hard work. A day's ploughing uses at least twice as much energy as working as a tailor or carpenter.[13] The work is carried out in the open air, in all weathers; it involves animals, which are unpredictable, difficult to control, and sometimes dangerous; it is arduous, even back-breaking, but also skilful, requiring the ability to use, maintain, and repair complex tools and machines. It is for these reasons that few country-dwellers have the romantic view of farm life which so many city-dwellers came to have in the nineteenth and twentieth centuries; farm work is far from a pastoral idyll.

Until the middle of the nineteenth century, countrywomen and children, as well as men, had little option but to work in the fields. Children, typically, worked full-time, for a twelve-hour day, from the age of 9 or 10, although girls might instead go into service as housemaids or cooks until they were married. In the West of England in 1843, women and children were 'working in the hay and corn harvests or in the dairy; hoeing turnips; weeding and picking stones; planting and digging potatoes; pulling, digging and hacking turnips; beating manure; filling dung carts; planting beans' and many were described by doctors as suffering from overwork, particularly in the dairy. In Lincolnshire, children as young as 5 and 6 were employed in gangs, contracted by a gang-master to a farmer who had dispensed with most of his workforce.[14]

By the 1870s and 1880s, there had been some improvements in that child labour did not then begin at so early an age, but typically at 11 or 12. However, the gang system continued in use; it was particularly pernicious in that labourers sometimes had to walk for one or two hours before and after their work, as farmers had destroyed—or, evocatively, 'tumbled down'—farm cottages to reduce the burden of local taxes. By the 1890s and 1900s, the labour of women and children was diminishing, although by no means extinct; it was particularly likely that they would work at harvest times or in such activities as hop-picking, but the Royal Commission on Labour in 1893–4 found women and children employed in gangs in Cambridgeshire, setting potatoes, hoeing and weeding corn, and haymaking. Women were still extensively employed in Northumberland, but in Somerset, where there was alternative work for women in glove and shirt making, the labour force was almost entirely male.

But farm work remained arduous for men as well as for women and children. The conversion of arable to pasture or to market gardening gave little relief; milking cows or weeding vegetables is as hard as ploughing, sowing, and harvesting corn, and takes place day-in, day-out throughout the year. There can have been few farm labourers who did not long for machines to do their work. But agriculture was and is difficult to mechanize, because few farming operations involve the repetition of simple tasks.

Despite this difficulty, a number of farming operations were mechanized before 1914. There were particular advantages for farmers in mechanizing the grain harvest; grain had to be cut when it was ripe and bound with string into sheaves, then gathered into stooks and dried in the fields and finally stacked until it was ready to be threshed. Each process except the last, threshing, had to be carried out as rapidly as possible, in case bad weather came, and there was thus great but temporary demand for labour; this arose particularly because, at a time when most farms combined grain production with animal husbandry, there was little scope for sharing labour between farms, since care of the animals also had to be fitted into the working day.

The last part of the harvesting process was the first to be mechanized. Threshing, carried out hitherto by beating the grain with flails, had been an autumn and winter task, employing women and children at a time when other jobs were scarce. The advent of threshing machines, which could move from farm to farm with their own crew of workers, destroyed that winter employment and led to distress in the major grain-growing areas; the hostility which this caused meant that the machines were often attacked in the Swing Riots of 1830–1. But the advent of steam-power, whereby an acre's yield of wheat could be threshed in 0.8 man-days as compared to 5 man-days by hand, settled the issue.

More significant, however, was the mechanization of reaping, not only because of its long-term consequences but because the diffusion of this new technology offers an insight into the nature of economic change in British farming. Although the first reapers had been used in British fields before 1851, it was the appearance of several American models at the Great Exhibition which brought them to general attention. Their potential to mechanize the cutting of grain was obvious, but when they were applied to British fields several models came rapidly to grief; they had been designed for the American prairies and could not cope with British terrain. It took over twenty years before even half of British grain was cut by machine, much less than after the same period in the United States.

Although the causes of this delay remain in dispute, it seems that the speed of diffusion was governed—as economic theory predicts that it should be—by the relative costs of using the new and the old technology.[15] As the reapers were improved and modified to suit British conditions—over 300 patents were taken out in Britain by competing manufacturers between 1850 and 1870[16]—and as agricultural wages rose, it became progressively more sensible to use reapers rather than men with scythes and sickles. Reapers were first introduced on the larger farms, where they could be fully employed throughout the harvest season.

Then, in the late 1870s, the technology progressed further with the introduction of the reaper and binder, mechanizing two jobs rather than just one; because of the cost savings which they offered, particularly at a time of rapidly falling grain prices, the new machines were introduced very rapidly. With their aid, an acre of wheat could be harvested with 0.5 man-days of labour, against 4.8 man-days with a sickle, and 2.4 man-days with a scythe.[17] By the 1880s, the reaper and binder was a universal feature of the British harvest, as it was to remain—although later pulled by a tractor rather than horses—until the introduction of the combine harvester after the Second World War.

As specialization increased and more land was turned over to animals, there was a need to examine methods of work there also. The first milking machines were introduced and farm buildings were redesigned. But farm work remained very hard, even after these changes; moreover, despite the increases in pay gained by farm workers, it remained one of the lowest paid of British occupations. Many young people were attracted, or fled, from the land and it became common—though it was always an exaggeration—to believe that agricultural labour was the preserve of older men. The supposed consequence, that the army would no longer be able to rely on strong young men from the farms but would be forced back on the puny products of the cities, became a matter of national concern between the South African and the First World wars. The truth was that, under the combined impact of agricultural depression, labour saving machinery and the rise of commerce and industry, agriculture had shrunk to virtual insignificance as an employer of labour by 1914. But that reduction in employment was combined with an adaptability to new economic circumstances, on the part of both labourers and farmers, which ensured that the productivity of British agriculture remained in 1914, as it had been throughout the nineteenth century, among the highest in the world. That achievement was to play a major role in ensuring Britain's victory in the ensuing world war.

7

MANUFACTURING

The factory of the world

In *The Workshop of the World*, J. D. Chambers described the rise of manufacturing industry in Britain before 1880: it was a period when the workshop rather than the factory remained the predominant place of work and when traditional craft skills had not yet in many industries been replaced by a new industrial technology. By 1914, by contrast, there were few areas of manufacturing which had not been touched by mass production within a factory context, although there remained many areas of craft skills and of specialized production, as there still are today. But if, in the title of this section, 'factory' rightly replaces 'workshop', the remaining words are still appropriate; Britain continued to provide manufactures for the world. Twenty-five per cent of world exports of manufactured goods were made in Britain, a percentage that was rivalled by only two countries, Germany and the United States. Even in 1914, Britain far surpassed them both in the proportion of the population engaged in manufacturing.

'Factory' is, however, probably a misleading word to use to describe the working environment of most British people employed in manufacturing before 1914. It conjures up a picture of a large group of buildings, noisy and dirty, occupied by machinery turning out standardized products and worked by a labour force which is predominantly semi-skilled, managed by (and often in conflict with) capitalist entrepreneurs, and subject to strict work discipline and rigid wage systems. While some of these features applied to some industries, few applied to all. Nor was there a clear or universal transition from workshop before 1850 or 1880 to factory by 1914. There are many ways of looking at the transitions which did occur; the most common is to examine the changing technology, but this cannot be divorced from changes in the respective roles of workers and managers. Important also is the relationship of manufacturing with other parts of the economy, in particular with the service sector which supplied both finance and markets.

Employers, managers, and workers

The traditional image of the Victorian factory-owner is encapsulated by the phrase, spoken in a Yorkshire or Lancashire accent: 'There's trouble at t'mill.' In other words, he—and it was certainly always a man—owned a textile mill in the North of England, over which he ruled with a rod of iron, calling in the police or, in extremity, the militia, to cow a recalcitrant workforce. That workforce, again in the traditional image, saw the factory as a 'dark, Satanic mill', to which men, women and children were bound by the impersonal forces of wage labour, their pride in old craft skills having been beaten out of them by the relentless march of the machine. They were always ranged, therefore, in opposition to the factory-owner, even to that rare employer who built model cottages or did not pay starvation wages, for such a man was abused, if not as a slave-driver, then as 'paternalist'.

Although Victorian manufacturing certainly experienced bitter industrial disputes, most employees never worked for such an employer. This was so partly because manufacturing remained small in scale. Information about the labour force of firms is difficult to obtain, but some voluntary answers to questions in the 1851 census show that, of 727,468 'men' whose 'master' answered the question, half were employed by masters with fewer than thirty employees. Even in 1907, when the first Census of Production was taken, the average firm was still small; the largest 100 firms of all types each had over 4,000 employees, but together accounted for only 1,420,667 workers, of whom over one-seventh worked for the largest enterprise, the General Post Office. The largest manufacturing firm in 1907, Fine Cotton Spinners and Doublers, employed only 30,000.[1] These large employers collectively employed only 7.9 per cent of the British labour force.

Moreover, large enterprises were heavily concentrated in a few industries, mostly outside manufacturing. Of the top 20 employers in 1907, 11 were railways; all the remainder, apart from the Post Office, were engaged in textiles, engineering, armaments, iron and steel, or shipbuilding.[2] This concentration was true also of the capital employed, although the range of industries was slightly different. Even in 1905, after a phase of company creation and merger from the middle of the 1890s, only 52 British manufacturing firms had capital of over £1,900,000. They were led by Imperial Tobacco, whose trade is self-explanatory, by the brewers Watney, Combe, Reid, and by the textile and sewing cotton makers, J. & P. Coats. Of the top 52, 17 were brewers, 10 were textile manufacturers, 9 came from the complex of iron, steel, shipbuilding and armaments firms, and 4 from chemicals and soap making. Other large firms, not included in this list of 52, could be found principally in the transport industries. Moreover, many of these large firms were the result of mergers between several smaller and competing firms, mergers which were unwieldy and often unstable, but meant that individual workers continued to work in small units, in factories or workshops scattered across the country. The largest single factory in Britain before 1914 was probably Armstrong Whitworth's engineering and armaments factory on Tyneside, employing at least 17,310 people in 1901, but this was very much an exception.[3]

Most of the largest firms had to grow in size and to attract outside investors by floating their shares on the Stock Exchange because of their need to use, and therefore to buy or build, expensive and complex equipment which was, in the economist's jargon, 'lumpy'. That is, one needed to buy or build a lot of it or none at all; three-quarters of a chemical plant or a railway which does not reach its destination is of no use. But this imperative did not apply to most industries, which remained dependent on small-scale equipment and where it therefore remained possible for an entrepreneur to begin 'in a small way of business' and to hope gradually to expand. This was true even in an industry like engineering, heavily dependent by the end of the nineteenth century on the use of machines, but where purchasing a number of basic machine-tools was not beyond the reach of an ambitious young mechanic. It was possible also to rent space, with power to go with it. There were few 'barriers to entry' in such industries and, as a result, new firms were constantly formed to meet market demands. Often, their founders were over-ambitious and the firms failed, so that many industries were in a constant state of flux; the average age of about 200 firms in the machine-tool-making industry in the 1880s was only about ten years and this rose to only about fifteen years by 1913.[4] Newer industries such as bicycle making and automobile production showed similar characteristics.

Small firms and short-lived firms imply a relationship between master and man very different from the caricature with which this section began; the worker is not akin to a machine, one interchangeable with another, but instead is a vital and individual contributor to the success of the firm. The state of technology also meant that employers relied on a high degree of skill on the part of the labour force. This was true in traditional craft industries which were little touched by mechanization or industrialization, but it applied also in the newer machine-using industries in which skill and dexterity was required to use the machines; sometimes, indeed, physical strength was needed as well, as in the engineering works where the manager mentioned that the workman needed to know when to throw his weight on the machine to stabilize it.

Even in the 'factory' industries characterized by large scale and the use of new technology, however, management was a matter of complex and slowly changing relationships between employer and employee. In many parts of the textile industries, for example, the first half of the nineteenth century saw the replacement of outwork—a subcontract system in which the entrepreneur supplied raw materials to be processed by workers in their own houses and workshops—by the concentration of production in the factory. But the management of the factory continued for the rest of the century to rely heavily on other forms of subcontracting, in which the organization of work and often indeed the employment of workers remained in the hands of foremen or skilled workers, sometimes incorporated into complex controls exercised through trade unions. The entrepreneur or manager did not, therefore, exert direct authority on the workforce as a whole, but managed through relationships with a much smaller number of crucial employees; this relationship was perforce much more one of co-operation than of coercion.

Sometimes, of course, things went wrong, most spectacularly in the major strikes or lockouts which punctuated the history of most of the major British industries. An early example was the coal miners' strike in north-eastern England in 1844, which collapsed after four months, but the late nineteenth century was punctuated by bitter disputes in textiles, mining, engineering, and other industries. Some were specific to their industries, the product for example of rapid technological change requiring adaptation of working practices, while others, such as the wave of labour unrest in Edwardian England, seem to have stemmed from more generalized declines in living standards.

While the last years of the nineteenth century saw increasing discussion of systematic and 'scientific' management and the importation into some British industries of time and motion studies, personnel departments and long managerial hierarchies, such developments were gradual and uneven. As one historian of work puts it, 'It was only after the First World War that the emphasis on monopoly, scale, and sophisticated labour management became marked.'[5] Before then, fluidity in industrial structure, small-scale production, and a close relationship between employer and employee was much more characteristic of British industry.

Innovations in products and in processes

Together, employers and employees had to cope, in the second half of the nineteenth century, with an unprecedented amount of innovation. Economists divide innovations into two types: product innovation, in which a new product is introduced, and process innovation, in which an old product is made in a new way. Product innovation is more dramatic; the invention and bringing into use of the bicycle, electric light, photography, or the reaper and binder dominate accounts of technological change after 1830. New products, drawn and described in loving detail in the catalogues of shops and manufacturers, fascinated the Victorians; they were displayed and celebrated in the numerous international exhibitions, beginning with the Great Exhibition of 1851, which were held in most of the developed nations between 1850 and 1914. New products were also personalized or personified in the figure of the great inventor, among them the Whitworth screw, Beecham's pills, and the Edison lamp.

But it was process innovation which contributed most to economic growth. Most important of all, probably, but most elusive and difficult to describe, were the improvements in manufacturing methods which came simply from the greater experience and skill of the workforce. The Victorians had a tendency, derided at the time and since but still very powerful in the development of vocational training, to value direct experience on the shop floor above book learning. They demanded, at least in theory, that even the boss's son should start by sweeping the factory floor, and resisted therefore the creation of a managerial class, scientifically trained in engineering or chemistry. Professional qualifications were to be earned by experience, not by studying at a university; often, this was by means of a 'premium' apprenticeship, a boy's parents paying a fee for him to learn from an experienced engineer or surveyor. Craft skills were acquired by normal apprenticeships, through years spent watching and imitating a master-craftsman.

Such methods of training ultimately proved inadequate, when no amount of experience could compensate for a lack of scientific knowledge of the behaviour of metals under stress or the exact properties of a chemical reaction. But the stress on practical experience did recognize the fact that product innovation, the germ of an idea which may one day turn into a marketable product, depends on a constant process of refinement and improvement, often carried out by the worker on the shop floor, who uses his skill and experience to achieve the best method of manufacture. 'Learning by doing' turned many a vague notion into a product which swept the world.

Such improvements are sometimes called 'disembodied technical change' because they are not expressed in a particular machine or piece of equipment. But there was also much 'embodied' process innovation in the nineteenth century. The most obvious examples are the growth of interchangeable parts and the development of new sources of motive power. Of the latter, it is the magic of steam which has come for many to symbolize the new technology of industrialization.

Steam is magic; it seemed so to the Victorians and it has remained so for their descendants. That boiling water could drain mines, drive textile machinery, and ultimately pull men and women in railway carriages so fast that, it was thought, they would be blinded by the rush of wind, was as unfathomable to men and women of the early nineteenth century as satellite television or the information superhighway created by fibre optics are to many people today. The magic of steam stemmed also from its adaptability to so many different uses.

The magic of the conjuror rarely survives an explanation of his tricks and the impact of steam has been somewhat blunted as historians have pointed out how it came only slowly into use and affected only parts of British industry. It is certainly true that before 1830, in the 'classical period' of the British Industrial Revolution, steam did little that was not, or could not have been, done by water power. The famous innovations in cotton and woollen textile manufacturing, for example, were all developed for use with human, animal, or water power and it was only in the 1830s and 1840s that steam was widely applied in the textile industries.

Nevertheless, the speed with which steam was brought into use in British industry was spectacular, even if the details are still uncertain. It is probable that, in 1840, less than 350,000 of steam horsepower was in use (though this was already double the estimated figure for 1800), but the figure by the 1870s was at least 2 million horsepower, about half of it in the textile industry. By 1907, a further 8 million horsepower had been installed. Over the same period, water power dropped to insignificant amounts, although it still provided 100,000 horsepower in the 1870s. Electrical generating capacity rose to 1.56 million horsepower in 1907, beginning the growth which was to take it to well over 100 million horsepower in the 1980s. The rate of growth of electricity in the twentieth century has been much more rapid than that of steam in the nineteenth, but the latter was, of course, mainly for industrial power while electricity was used for lighting and domestic heating and cooking as well.[6]

The 'age of steam' brought with it, however, disadvantages both for industrial workers and the population as a whole. For workers, the main problem lay with the transmission of power from the steam engine to the individual machines; the only method, in a textile or engineering factory with many machines, perhaps laid out on several floors, was to take the power to each room via a thick leather belt running on large overhead pulleys and thence down, on smaller belts, to pulley-wheels on each machine. The noise was horrendous. In a room with many machines, the belts cut out much of the light. Changes of speed could be achieved only by shifting the belt from one pulley-wheel to another, a process which put additional strain on a belt which was stitched together and yet running at several hundred revolutions per second. If not well maintained, belts broke, the ends whipping across the machine room with severe danger to anyone in the way. For the wider population, smoke from industrial steam engines added to the pollution from coal fires which blackened first the northern industrial cities and then all towns and cities by the middle of the twentieth century.

Electricity ultimately reduced this wider pollution, but had previously improved conditions within the factory. Although initially electricity was used to drive a motor and thus the belts from a central source, the development of individual electric motors attached to each machine greatly reduced the danger and noise while adding to the flexibility of work because of the greater ability to vary machine speeds. These advantages brought a rapid advance of electricity into British industry in the twentieth century, but in 1907 only just over 10 per cent of total power in industry was electrical.[7] Meanwhile, by the end of the nineteenth century, electric lighting was beginning to replace gas.

As with all innovations, the speed with which these process changes were diffused varied from industry to industry and from firm to firm. There were similar variations in the speed with which industries and firms adopted new products for manufacture and sale. Trade journals, describing individual factories, document these variations and therefore the range within each industry from 'best practice' to 'worst practice'; such a range is to be expected, but what came increasingly to be alleged was that British industries, as a whole, were failing to keep up with international best practice and therefore failing to maintain their lead in manufacturing.

The growth of foreign competition in manufacturing

From the point of view of the British consumer, the development of manufacturing capacity in many overseas countries, led by Germany, France, and the United States, brought many benefits. To the extent that Britain, in the middle of the nineteenth century, was close to being a monopoly producer of many manufactured goods, the growth of foreign competition increased the range of choice and reduced the prices which British consumers had to pay. It was to obtain these benefits, and those from cheaper agricultural goods, that from the 1840s, Britain became the principal advocate of 'free trade' and of the abolition of tariffs on the import of goods produced or made abroad. As a result of this policy, British women could decorate themselves and their houses with Chinese silks bought at Liberty of London,

British farmers could harvest with the aid of American reaping machinery, and British children could feast on tinned corned beef from Argentina or bananas from Central America.

British manufacturing, and ultimately the consumers of its products, benefited also from foreign product and process innovations. The electric light bulb or the milling machine from the United States, aniline dyes to produce colour-fast textiles from Germany, the daguerreotype—an early form of photograph—from France represented a tiny fraction of the new products which came into British markets from abroad and which British manufacturers could seek to use, imitate, or improve; similarly, German and American development of the use of electric power or the diesel engine led to process innovation in Britain. Even if some reports in the British press of the successes of industry overseas were doom-laden, those successes were publicized so that British manufacturers could adopt or adapt foreign techniques to British conditions or, sometimes, reject them as unsuitable to British raw materials or the skills of British labour. One of the earliest and most influential accounts was the report in 1855 on 'The American System of Manufactures', but it was followed by many others.[8]

British manufacturers and British consumers were quick to take advantage of these new opportunities. In constant prices of 1913 (so adjusting for changes in prices), British imports of finished manufactures rose from £4.2 million in 1830 to £7.9 million in 1850, £36.9 million in 1870, £71.6 million in 1890, and £155.6 million in 1913, roughly doubling every twenty years; there were similar increases in the imports of raw materials to be used by British industry, from £50.8 million in 1830 to £328.3 million in 1913. These increases in the overall volume of imports only hint, of course, at the enormous increase in variety and range of products, and thus of consumer choice, which underlie them. There can have been no one in Britain in 1913 who had not benefited.

It is surprising, in view of this, that most of the discussion of these developments has been cast in pessimistic terms, with the emphasis placed on the damage which increased imports did to the British economy. The alarm was first sounded at the Paris Exhibition of 1867, when it became clear that the British lead in manufactured goods, so clear at the Crystal Palace in 1851, was being challenged in some, though not many, fields by the products of the United States, France, and Germany. As exhibition succeeded exhibition, prophecies of doom increased in volume and rampant xenophobia characterized such publications as *Made in Germany*, which described the invasion of German goods and called for the return of protection for British industry.[9] More recently, much history written since the 1950s has placed the increase in foreign competition in the late Victorian period within the context of a wider debate about the 'decline of the British economy'.

It is natural that individual manufacturers should feel upset or aggrieved if their product is bettered or their market invaded by a foreign competitor; many of the protests about the rise of imports of manufactures came from industries or firms in such a position. In some cases, they could argue that the competition was unfair and that the British government should intervene to see fair play; such was the case when British West Indian sugar, produced after the emancipation of the slaves, had to compete with the products of the slave states of Cuba and Brazil. Later in the century, British manufacturers who faced imports unaffected by tariffs could argue that they were at a disadvantage when the home markets of their competitors were protected; they usually forgot, in their protests, to acknowledge that they benefited from raw materials also imported free of tariffs. Even when this was not so, British consumers probably benefited from the 'unfair' competition and it was a task for government to decide how to balance the interests of producers and consumers of each product. But in many other cases, British consumers could benefit either from the greater inventiveness or skill of foreign producers or simply from the fact that the climate or the availability of raw materials gave foreigners an advantage over British producers. In such cases, foreign imports could destroy a British industry, leaving entrepreneurs, managers and workers to seek some other occupation.

The interest of consumers as a whole lies in maximizing the overall output of the economy. This requires that everyone, consumers and producers alike, behaves sensibly, seeking by their actions to produce and consume as efficiently as possible. Foreign trade is part of this, a means by which one country exchanges goods which it can make well for the goods of another country, which that country can make relatively better. In these terms, it would only be reasonable to blame British manufacturers for failing to respond to foreign competition, if it could be shown that British manufacturing was systematically less efficient than foreign manufacturing, perhaps because British factories were systematically less well equipped or less well managed than those overseas or if British society was so organized that it systematically produced the wrong goods. The word 'systematically' is used three times to emphasize the fact that more evidence is needed than examples drawn from individual industries.

As was argued in discussing the performance of the economy as a whole in Chapter 1, it has proved to be difficult to identify such evidence of a systematic failure in British manufacturing. There were certainly individual failures, where at the extreme an entrepreneur made misjudgements resulting in bankruptcy, or where an individual firm was slow to invest in new machinery or was taken by surprise by a new competitor. But studies of British industries as diverse as textiles, engineering, and iron and steel during the late nineteenth century have shown that, on average, industrialists responded sensibly and reasonably quickly to what are called 'market signals': the prices of labour and machinery, the opportunities for sales and the changing requirements of governments. It is difficult to ask for more.

The skills of industrialists and industrial workers

Even if individual entrepreneurs responded sensibly to the pressures and opportunities which crowded in upon them in Britain in the late nineteenth century, it remains possible that society as a whole was so organized as to hamper their efforts and to reduce the rate of growth of the economy. One possible cause of such a societal bias, which was identified at the time and has often since been studied, was the system of education and training. That system and its results in terms of the quality of the labour force affected, of course, much more than manufacturing industry, but it is there that many observers have alleged that its deficiencies were most apparent.

The central allegation is that the British educational system produced a labour force which was, at all levels, less well-educated and less skilled than it could have been. Levels of basic literacy, standards of technical training, and the inadequate numbers of graduates in science and technology have all been attacked, often through comparisons with other countries, in particular Germany. Even more fundamentally, the whole orientation of British society towards industry, influenced particularly by the education of the élite in the public schools, has been attacked in a way epitomized in the title of Martin Wiener's book *English Culture and the Decline of the Industrial Spirit*. The word 'English' is significant, since even the fiercest detractors recognize the excellence of Scottish education, even if the consequences of that excellence for the relative prosperity of the Scottish economy are obscure.

Wiener and others have argued that the entrepreneurial and inventive spirit of the Industrial Revolution was gradually transformed into a timid and unenterprising culture, ill-suited to the needs of the late nineteenth and twentieth centuries. The English 'cult of the amateur' was combined with a preference for practical experience over 'book learning' to produce throughout society a suspicion of the expert. Industry did not want to employ university-trained scientists or engineers or, if it did, insisted that they should begin work on the shop floor. Apprenticeship rather than school- or college-based technical training meant that even skilled workers lacked a fundamental understanding of the technologies with which they worked; all classes of society, therefore, were suspicious of new methods and unwilling to use new machines.

This set of allegations is certainly exaggerated. Other educational systems were very different from that of Britain; Germany, for example, put a much greater emphasis on vocational training. If most of a country's population was engaged in subsistence agriculture, it needed an educational system which would rapidly transform peasants into industrial workers. Britain, on the other hand, had a long tradition of craft and industrial training and, before state education, had achieved high levels of basic literacy. State education for the working classes emphasized the acquisition of basic skills, leaving the specific industrial training to the workplace; this could be done because that training was well developed, while in Germany it had to be underpinned by school or college classes. Moreover, British working men or women acquired a great deal of technical training in their own time, through evening classes which were the envy of many foreign observers and helped to promote an ideal of the British system, upward social mobility through self-help; this was an idea foreign to many European systems.

So far as the middle and upper classes are concerned, there is no doubt that, compared either to Germany or to the United States, British universities turned out many fewer chemists and engineers; this hampered the emergence of an industrial chemicals industry able to rival that of Germany. On the other hand, British civil and mechanical engineers, who had been trained as apprentices, remained in demand throughout the world; they built the railway systems and established the engineering capacity of much of the British Empire and even Latin America, where they had no imperial sway. The scions of the aristocracy or even the children of the middle classes were, it is true, slow to enter the management of manufacturing industry, unless it was to join the family firm. They preferred the learned professions, the Church, the army, or Civil Service, or the City, the growing complex of deposit and merchant banking, trading, and insurance which, by the late nineteenth century, was organizing trade and investment throughout the world. Amateurs they might be at the outset, since there was certainly no formal training in schools or universities for such work, but this did not inhibit their amassing fortunes which were larger and more frequently made there than in manufacturing. Meanwhile the British aristocracy continued to combine its high status with a healthy interest in new ways of making money.

More fundamentally, it seems unlikely that deficiencies in education can have been disastrous for entrepreneurship, management, and technical training in British industry. British manufacturing did not lag far behind that of Germany or the United States before 1914. This was partly because Britain was far ahead before 1830, but it is still difficult to imagine that, by rectifying any educational deficiencies, Britain could have stayed ahead. There were plenty of enterprising people; firms continued to be founded, new ideas tried out, and machinery and production methods learnt from other countries. British manufacturing could not be good at everything, but it was good at a great deal.

8

EXTRACTING

The fabric of everyday life

The symbol of industrial civilization is the machine; but machines are made from and operate upon raw materials. Similarly, urban civilization depends upon raw materials, with which towns and cities are built, lit, and cleaned and their citizens warmed and clothed. Thus the age of the machine and of the growth of the cities depended upon an immense expansion in the production, either in Britain or overseas, of raw materials; they were extracted often by much more primitive processes than were used in the factories or workshops in which the coal, iron, cotton, tin, lead, hemp—the list is endless—were turned into a multitude of finished goods.

The impact of buildings

Think of a single Victorian house, one of millions which have survived for a century or more in British towns and cities. The basic pattern was two rooms up, two rooms down, with a back extension to accommodate kitchen, scullery, and bathroom; a cellar; and an attic either for storage or to house child and servants. Brick was the main building material, with stone ornaments, but this was only the beginning of the materials, and the skills, which went into its construction. The extent of elaboration varied, of course, with the social class of the occupant, although at least one bay window adorned most houses by the end of the century. Outside there were intricate iron railings on the garden wall, quarry tiles on the front path, a front door with more or less complex mouldings surrounding stained-glass panels, wrought-iron guttering, stone sills and pillars. Inside there were moulded plaster cornices, hand- or machine-turned wooden doors, windows, and skirting boards, dado rails, heavy patterned wallpapers, marble or imitation-marble fireplaces, ornamented mirrors, polished floors, lead piping, all installed before the house was furnished or occupied.

At the other extreme of size, take the Crystal Palace built to house the Great Exhibition of 1851; the building, possibly the earliest example of prefabricated construction, contained 293,655 panes of glass, 330 iron columns and 24 miles of guttering.[1] In an early example of conservation engineering, the wooden fence panels which surrounded the building site were designed to be taken down and used as floorboards when the palace was complete. While these construction methods remained unusual, the growth of town halls, factories, and railway stations in Victorian and Edwardian England, built in increasingly ornate styles, brought ever-increasing demands for building materials; all had to be built, maintained, equipped, and furnished. In London, the building of the Victoria Embankment of the Thames between Westminster and Blackfriars bridges, for example, took 650,000 cubic feet of granite, 80,000 cubic yards of brick, 140,000 cubic yards of concrete, 500 cubic feet of timber, 2,000 tons of iron, and 125,000 square feet of York paving.[2] A particular demand came from the country houses of the wealthy; Brodsworth Hall in Yorkshire, including its park, gardens, and furniture cost £60,000 in 1863, Adcote in Shropshire £30,000 in 1881.[3]

But if we take just the simple house at the moment of its completion, we can think back to the materials and skills which have gone into its building, think forward to the needs of its occupants for fuel, furniture, and other materials and, last, multiply both those by 5.2 million, the number of houses built in Britain between 1856 and 1980 (on top of the 3.4 million houses in England and Wales and an unknown number in Scotland which already existed in 1851).[4] As the population increased and with it the houses in which it lived, demand increased at a rapid rate for a plethora of materials, furnishings, and interior decorations. One simple but striking example is that, after the paper industry exploited new technology to use woodpulp instead of rags as its raw material and after duties on paper largely vanished in the 1860s, British wallpaper production rose from 13.8 million yards in 1834 to 358.4 million yards in 1874.[5]

As catalogues of Victorian building supplies make clear, many of the materials which were used were supplied prefabricated, but putting them together and undertaking the many tasks, such as bricklaying and plastering, which could only be done on site, remained a complex and skilled operation, carried out by craftsmen who were accorded high status in working-class society. 'Masons and plumbers were regarded as the élite, followed by bricklayers and carpenters and joiners. . . . Each trade had its own pride and its own status . . .'[6] The impact of the building boom is partly reflected in its workers. The building trades together were one of the largest of occupations, rising from 376,000 men in 1841 to 1,140,000 in 1911 (at which point they ranked fifth after metal manufactures, commerce, agriculture, and mining and quarrying), while over 150,000 in 1841 and over 400,000 in 1911 produced 'wood, furniture, fittings and decorations, bricks, cement, pottery and glass'.[7] These were, in most cases, the finishing trades. They were supplied by workers in raw materials, the most prominent being those in 'Mining and Quarrying and Workers in the Products of Mines and Quarries' (218,000 in 1841 and 1,202,000 in 1911).

It was this growth in buildings, and in the people and consumption allied to buildings, together with the demand for industrial raw materials, which explains the expansion of so many of the extractive and materials-processing industries of Victorian Britain and, along with them, the expansion of imports of raw materials or partly processed goods. It also explains, less happily, the changed landscape and in some cases the dereliction of industrial Britain, as extractive industries flowered, and in some cases withered and died, under the influence of changing fashions and of foreign competition.

The industrial landscape

In the late eighteenth century, in the early years of the Industrial Revolution, men and women looked with a mixture of awe and horror at the impact of industrialization upon the countryside. The two emotions were always mixed, for despite concern at smoky furnaces and gaping quarries, there was pride at what man could now wreak upon nature. Anna Seward wrote in 1785 of Coalbrookdale, site of the first iron bridge and in many ways the symbol of the new Iron Age. She described how

> ... thy grassy lanes, thy wildwood glens,
> Thy knolls and bubbling wells, thy rocks and streams,

had been transformed; now

> ... red the countless fires
> With umber'd flames, bicker on all thy hills,
> Dark'ning the Summer's sun with columns large,
> Of thick, sulphureous smoke, which spread, like palls,
> That screen the dead, upon the sylvan robe
> Of thy aspiring rocks; pollute thy gales,
> And stain thy glassy waters.[8]

By the middle of the nineteenth century, however, 'the sublime and the picturesque' aspects of early industrialization had yielded to the march of the cities and the smoke of the factory chimneys. William Wordsworth lived long enough to make the transition himself. He wrote in 1787–9 of quarrymen:

> Some (hear you not their chisel's clinking sound?)
> Toil, small as pigmies, in the gulf profound;
> Some, dim between th'aereal cliffs descry'd,
> O'erwalk the viewless plank from side to side;
> Rocks that ceaseless ring
> Glad from their airy baskets hang and sing.[9]

but, by 1814, industrialization was symbolized by:

> ... a huge town, continuous and compact,
> Hiding the face of earth for leagues. ...
> O'er which the smoke of unremitting fires
> Hangs permanent, and plentiful as wreathes
> Of vapour glittering in the morning sun.[10]

By 1844, the year in which he published *The Old Curiosity Shop*, Dickens had no doubt of the impact of industry on the environment; Little Nell, the heroine, saw in Wolverhampton '. . . a cheerless region, where not a blade of grass was seen to grow, where not a bud put forth its promises in the spring; where nothing green could live but on the surface of the stagnant pools, which here and there lay idly sweltering by the black roadside.'[11]

Few parts of Britain were unaffected, for the complex geology of the country means that a multiplicity of minerals lie beneath the surface; most were exploited in the nineteenth century. For example, Cornwall, Britain's westernmost county whose economy is now oriented to agriculture, fishing, and tourism, has been a centre of mining for tin and copper since Roman times. The Industrial Revolution saw a great expansion of mining operations, aided by the use of 'Cornish engines'—steam beam engines used to pump water out of the mines—and the creation of a characteristic landscape of mine buildings and pumping-engine houses across large areas of the county, some spectacularly sited on the rocky coasts. By the 1870s, both copper and tin mining was in decline in the face of exhausted seams and foreign competition from areas such as Malaya, and the dereliction which can be seen today began. The Cornish landscape was also scarred by the digging of vast pits to satisfy the demands from the Staffordshire pottery industry and, increasingly, foreign purchasers, for kaolin for the manufacture of china. Pits are interspersed with huge, glistening white, spoil-heaps of quartz and mica washed from the kaolin. Eight tons of spoil have to be dumped for each ton of kaolin produced, and the result now dominates the landscape of southern Cornwall.

A second example is that of the Swansea Valley in South Wales, which became the centre of world production of copper during the third quarter of the nineteenth century on the basis of ores imported from the mines of Cornwall and Anglesey. By the First World War, however, the industry had virtually disappeared from Swansea, superseded by production close to the mines of Chile and the United States. In its heyday, however, the copper smelting spawned a huge variety of by-products. Gases from the process were used to produce sulphuric acid, further by-products from which were copper sulphate, exported to treat European vines against the devastations of phylloxera, hydrochloric acid, bleaching powder, and soda. The expertise gained in copper smelting was transferred to other raw materials such as nickel, cobalt, silver, and gold. In almost all cases, the processes gave rise to spoil-heaps which spread across the landscape.

Lead mining was another substantial activity in nineteenth-century Britain, declining like copper and tin under the impact of imports at the end of the century but thriving before then as a result of the demands of the building industry for pipework and plumbing and for paint, based on red or white lead. Production of the crystal glass which became very popular in Victorian Britain depended on the addition of lead, which was also used to adulterate bread and even wine. Highly poisonous both in processing and in use, lead was mined in the North of England, North Wales, Shropshire, and Somerset and processed in many of these areas in flues dug into the hillsides, stretching up to two miles in length from a furnace.

The extraction of building materials was even more widespread and had an even greater impact on the environment. Since stone can be found across the country and is expensive to transport, quarries were opened up in many areas. Bricks became the great building material of the second half of the nineteenth century, particularly after the removal of taxes on bricks in 1850 and the invention of machinery for making pressed bricks about 1856. Before then, bricks had been handmade from clays, dug by hand, which were found only in relatively few parts of the country, but pressed bricks could be made from harder clays, shales, and marls found in the Midlands and North of England. It was only gradually and as a result of technological changes in the late nineteenth century that large-scale brickworks in such areas as Bedfordshire became sufficiently profitable. Glassworks, too, were widely established. Other materials were found only in particular parts of the country, such as the Welsh slate which became the cheapest roofing material in Britain and whose production led to the enormous and dramatic slate quarries of North Wales.

The extraction and processing of minerals and raw materials disfigured the countryside, while the smells could pollute large areas. In 1862, the Select Committee on Noxious Vapours found that the worst damage was done by the manufacturers of soda, sulphuric acid, and ammonia salts and by the smelting of copper and lead. In St Helen's the alkali works killed trees, while the waste from lime and coal used in the manufacture of soda was dumped anywhere that could be found; 'a very offensive matter flows from it, a yellowish creamy looking matter, sometimes nearly black ... (which) completely destroys vegetation ...'[12] In the Swansea Valley, which was devastated by copper smelting, the countryside around 'which is subjected to the direct and concentrated influence of the copper smoke, is entirely denuded of vegetation, the hill sides have not a blade of grass upon them, but are converted into a mass of debris of gravel and stones.' The Commissioners found that copper smoke was converted by moisture into vitriol. In North Liverpool, the manufacture of hydrochloric acid produced such fumes that it drove the 'more respectable inhabitants' out of Everton; their 'good residences' were being pulled down and 'streets of small houses', whose future inhabitants had less choice, were being built on the land.

Coal

By far the largest of the extractive industries, and also the most widespread within Britain, was coal, the foundation of what Asa Briggs, following Lewis Mumford, so memorably calls 'carboniferous capitalism'.[13] Demand for coal came both from domestic consumers, to burn in the millions of new hearths and ovens, and from industry; its use there was not only to fuel steam engines— a small part of total demand—but as fuel in the processing of many other minerals. In addition, the growth of steam shipping led, by the end of the nineteenth century, to very substantial demand for 'bunkers', coal stocks held around the world to fuel ships.

Consumption of coal in Britain had risen gradually over many centuries and in 1830 was about 30 million tons per annum.[14] Just over one-third, at that time, was for domestic use, principally for heating, while the iron and steel industry was the second largest user. About 7 per cent of domestic consumption was in London, and much of the rest in large towns and cities which were remote from almost all the mining areas; it was also sometimes cheaper to take coal to other raw materials rather than vice versa. The transport of coal was therefore itself a major activity, occupying thousands of coastal sailors and canal boatmen. Some canals were built mainly for this purpose. With the rapid growth of the railways in the 1830s, however, the carriage of coal became one of the main activities of many railway companies and stimulated fierce competition and the building of branch lines and coal yards in many areas. Rail gradually replaced coastal shipping as the main means of transport, although shipping enjoyed a revival at the end of the century.

What is most striking, however, is the overall growth in coal consumption; coal was said as early as 1865 to be 'the staple produce of the country'.[15] Thirty million tons in 1830 was replaced by 189.4 million tons in 1913, with a further 98 million tons exported. Coal output, in other words, rose by nine-and-a-half times while the British population increased by five times. By 1913, industrial and commercial use far outstripped the domestic uses: iron and steel took 12 per cent, other industries 23 per cent and the railways 5 per cent, while domestic use accounted for 12 per cent, although much of the 4 per cent consumed by the gas industry must have ended up as domestic lighting, heating, and cooking. Exports and the provision of bunkers for shipping also rose rapidly, particularly at the end of the century, so that over 30 per cent of British coal went overseas in 1913.

Coal production and distribution touched the whole of Britain. There were major coalfields in Kent, in south-west England, in South and North Wales, in the west and east Midlands, in Lancashire, Cheshire, Yorkshire, Cumberland, Northumberland, and Durham, and in central Scotland. Each coalfield produced coal with particular chemical advantages and disadvantages, so much so that it was not really an homogeneous product; 'to the dealer in coal it is only the name of a whole class of substances, and . . . means about as much as the words "cloth" and "paper"'.[16] As a result, the fortunes of individual coalfields waxed and waned with the products made with or from coal; by the twentieth century, coal was an ingredient of, among other things, 'dye-stuffs, pigments, perfumes, medicines, disinfectants, explosives and photographic materials'.[17] Meanwhile coal of different types criss-crossed the country in search of profitable markets. Sometimes, of course, the process was reversed, when it was sensible to transport other raw materials, such as iron or copper, close to the coalfields.

Despite the growth in the scale and range of industries dependent on coal, the technologies which were used to get the mineral were primitive and slow to change, little different from those which had been used for centuries. The immense expansion of production often depended, therefore, on a similar expansion of the numbers of people employed. Thus while output of coal in Britain expanded by about 9.4 times, the numbers in the industry employed rose by 9.8 times from 115,100 in 1831 to 1,127,900 in 1913.[18] (A potent example of the rise and fall of industries is the fact that at the beginning of 1995, when the coal mining industry was privatized, it employed only 7,000 men.)

Although the course of productivity change in mining is more complex than appears from these figures, coal mining remained even by 1913 largely a matter of pick and shovel, with coal-cutting machinery installed in only a small minority of pits. Miners, one of the élite groups within Britain's working class, still scrabbled for a living in tiny tunnels amidst dirt and dust and with an ever-present fear of explosion or accident. There had certainly been improvements, most notably in the prohibition of women and children from working underground, but in most pits conditions remained deplorable, with employers resisting even requests for pithead baths in which miners could wash before walking home.

There were few controls on colliery owners; it took many years to enforce reasonable safety standards within the mines, but mine owners retained the freedom to 'externalize the social costs of coal mining by disfiguring the landscape and indirectly by damaging the national health'.[19] The vast quantities of coal-waste were burnt at the pithead or piled up in enormous tips. Coal was washed in local rivers and streams, turning them black and, in times of flooding, depositing a thin layer of coal dust over fields and meadows. Water pumped from mines into rivers contained an excess of sulphuric acid which, if used in steam engines, could corrode the boilers and lead to explosions. Coke production from coal had devastating effects; it was said in 1878 that, in the vicinity of coking plants, '. . . the growth of trees is checked or destroyed, fences are killed, crops of every description are injured, cattle suffer and wool is made almost useless'.[20] The Northumberland and Durham coalfield was well described in 1862 as 'this great district of subterranean darkness and superficial blackness'.[21]

However, it was domestic soot that did the most widespread damage as Roy Church, the historian of the British coal industry, makes clear. Urban industrial districts enjoyed perhaps 20 per cent less sunlight than rural areas, a likely cause of the rickets which disfigured many children and adults.[22] Coal fires deposited a fine layer of dust and ash throughout the house. Just after the First World War, at a time when the average annual income was about £100, over £1 per year was being spent on removing soot deposits in the average household. Another indication of the problem was *Rus in Urbe: or Flowers that Thrive in London Gardens or Smoky Towns*, the title of a book published in 1886.[23] The effects on buildings were insidious and it was not until the Clean Air Acts of the 1950s had reduced smoke pollution that it became economically feasible to clean stonework. Meanwhile, coal had literally blackened Britain.

9

NOT MAKING, DIGGING,
OR GROWING

The service sector

To Adam Smith in 1776, the work of a 'servant' was of no
account compared to that of a 'manufacturer': a servant, even so
respectable a servant of the public as the sovereign, 'adds to the
value of nothing', while a manufacturer 'adds generally to the
value of the materials which he works upon'.[1] Smith, a man of his
time, did not need to comment on the high value of agricultural
labour. Yet, within 150 years, the Industrial Revolution, of
which Smith saw the beginnings, had not only transformed the
work of manufacturers but had created, before 1914, a labour
force in which there were more 'servants' than 'manufacturers'.

Smith's distinction and judgement lives on in the late twentieth century in the rhetoric of politicians and businessmen who
assert that only the making (and possibly the growing) of things
can contribute to 'wealth creation' or to a positive balance of
payments. Such an assertion ignores the evidence of their own
eyes and forgets that they and most of their constituents and
employees earn an honest living without making anything—or,
as economists' jargon puts it, any 'widgets'—from one year to
the next. Unfortunately, this foolishness has often been paralleled by historians who have relegated the growth of the 'service sector' of the economy, as it is now called, to a footnote
while lavishing several chapters upon manufacturing industry
or agriculture.

The matter is made worse by an aspect of British culture which is often commented upon by Americans; although Smith was careful to point out that the king 'with all the officers both of justice and war who serve under him' were servants of the public, most service is still regarded as 'menial'. Personal service, especially the work of domestic servants, waiters or cabdrivers, is now seen, as it was in the nineteenth century, as subservient, contrasted with the manly independence of craftsman or peasant; shopkeepers are portrayed as fawning on their customers, while even professional men, such as lawyers or doctors, are thought of as prostituting their knowledge and intellect by selling their services. Last, housework, the choice or lot of most wives in late Victorian Britain, is doubly devalued; not only is the work seen as 'domestic drudgery', it is unpaid.

In view of this, it is paradoxical that, in Britain as in every country which has experienced economic development, industrialization has created among consumers a greater and greater demand for non-material goods. Indeed, Britain led the way in building up the service sector as a proportion of its economy and labour force. Why is this? How was Britain in 1914 different from Britain in 1830 as a result? What was the effect on the lives of those who provided for those demands?

First, what do people in the service sector do? It is easiest to say that they do everything which is not manufacturing, mining or agriculture. As such, the service sector in the late nineteenth century included footballers, bankers, maids, parsons, shopkeepers, schoolteachers, railwaymen, and gravediggers, to name but a fraction of the 1.7 million employed in service occupations in 1841 or the 6.2 million in 1911. In broad groups, the pattern is shown separately for men and for women in Figures 9.1 and 9.2. The service sector had expanded immensely since the preindustrial period; as R. M. Hartwell has put it (though he omits domestic service): 'The great pre-industrial services were law, medicine and religion; the services which expanded most obviously with economic growth were transport, distribution, finance and government.'[2]

The simplest explanation for the expansion of these occupa-

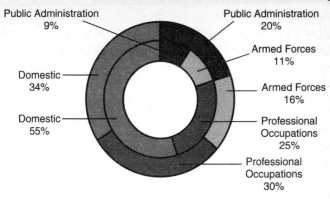

FIG. 9.1   Male service occupations, (inner) 1841 and (outer) 1911

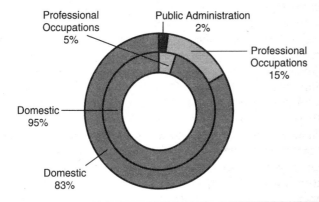

FIG. 9.2   Female service occupations, (inner) 1841 and (outer) 1911

tions within the economy is that there is a limit to the amount that people can eat. As incomes rose in the middle and late nineteenth century, and particularly as, from the 1860s, the price of food fell, first the upper and middle, and then most of the working, classes, found that they had sufficient to feed, clothe, and house themselves and their families and also some to spare. As economists put it, there is a low 'income elasticity of demand' for food as compared with other goods. As income rises, and after basic needs have been met, expenditure on food does not increase proportionately, although there can be more expenditure on higher quality and processed foods. The income elasticity of demand for houses, clothes, and other manufactured consumer goods is higher, but again there are limits, both physical and cultural, to the amount that can be spent on them. So the surplus increasingly went on services.

But this explanation is too simple. In spending more and more on services, people in the nineteenth, as in the twentieth, century were, first, taking advantage of the increasing specialization of the economy, one of the main benefits of economic growth and the Industrial Revolution. Second, they were also choosing leisure.

It is a caricature of a pre-industrial or isolated economy to believe that, in it, everybody provided for all their own wants, growing their own food, building and furnishing their own houses, making all their clothes and household goods. From the earliest times, there was specialization of production and distribution; some people made pots, some herded cattle, some traded far afield, others tilled the fields at home. But, even in the family economy of the early Industrial Revolution, in either town or country, the conjunction between home and work meant that the household was the focus of production and still provided a large proportion of its own goods and services.

A family forced by shipwreck to revert to the primitive economy was described in a favourite Victorian novel, *Swiss Family Robinson*, by Johann Wyss; it was first published in English in 1857 and pointed the contrast with the world as it had already become. By the end of the nineteenth century the specialization of the economy was far advanced; people might still make some of their own clothes, grow a few vegetables in the garden, keep a pig, do some of their own decorating or make their own jam, but many did none of these things. Instead, they bought them at a shop or employed a specialist. What resulted was a network of transport, wholesale and retail trade, tradesmen, and professionals to meet all these new needs and wants.

Simultaneously, growing incomes were spent in increased leisure and on the people who provided leisure services. The reduced working hours of the late nineteenth century, and in particular the extension of the weekend, gave opportunities to watch and play games, to attend theatres and music halls, to gamble and drink, all outside rather than inside the household. Perhaps most important of all, although some would dispute that this was a form of leisure, greater family incomes allowed women to do two jobs rather than three; they could now concentrate on unpaid housework and childcare rather than juggle the demands of paid work, children, and household tasks. This choice, sometimes presented as a means to the subjugation of women, was seen differently by the working-class women interviewed by Elizabeth Roberts; as she puts it: 'Women who worked full-time were certainly not regarded as emancipated by contemporaries, rather as drudges. Women whose husbands earned sufficient money to clothe, feed and house the family preferred to have a reduced workload rather than extra income.'[3]

Skills and characteristics

Throughout the period from 1830 to 1914, the average employee in the service sector—excluding the professions and domestic service—was more productive than the average employee in manufacturing industry. In 1856, when the first rough estimates can be made, labour productivity (measured for example as the total spent on the service divided by the number employed) in transport and communications was about two-and-a-half times, and in distribution three times, that in manufacturing. The gap soon began to shrink, but even in 1914, these service occupations were about one-and-a-half times as productive as manufacturing jobs.

In some occupations, especially in transport and communications, this may be because such workers used, in conjunction with their own efforts, very expensive capital equipment by comparison with that used in manufacturing. Railways cost a great deal to build and maintain, as do railway engines and other rolling stock. But even in commerce in general, where levels of plant and machinery were below those in factories, labour productivity was much higher. In other parts of the service sector, it is likely that doctors, lawyers or bankers were at least as productive as industrial managers, although the actual productivity of either group is extremely difficult to assess. Only in domestic and personal services is it likely that productivity was lower than in manufacturing.

A further (though neither entirely independent nor infallible) indication of relative levels of productivity is relative pay. In 1835 messengers and porters, police, guards and watchmen were paid about twice as much as agricultural or general labourers; indeed, though they were relatively unskilled, these service workers were paid as much as most skilled workers in manufacturing industry. Among the higher paid, clerks were paid almost four times as much as skilled industrial workers although teachers, then as always an undervalued profession, received only as much as a skilled man in engineering. Clergymen, surgeons, medical officers, engineers, and surveyors all received well above £200 per annum, certainly enough at that time to put them among the servant-keeping classes, although their pay was dwarfed, as always, by solicitors' and barristers' annual income of over £1,100.

By 1911, the differential in favour of the service trades had generally narrowed or even disappeared; messengers, porters, police, guards, and watchmen were by then paid less than general labourers, although agricultural labourers lagged far behind. Clerks and those in other white-collar occupations earned only twice as much as skilled industrial workers, while solicitors and barristers continued to lead the field, earning over £1,300.[4] Domestic servants, throughout the period, lagged behind. Living-in servants received so much of their income in board and lodging that it is difficult to make comparisons. In 1845, when the average working man was earning £20 a year, a household income of £100 a year was required to keep a single maid and, by the end of the century, to have a butler or footman necessitated an income of over £600.[5]

Over the course of the period, it is clear, service occupations as a whole lost some of the advantages in greater labour productivity and pay which they had enjoyed over manufacturing industry. First, there was an ever-increasing input of capital into manufacturing, so that factory workers were able to increase their productivity by the use of more, and more sophisticated, machinery. Second, with the spread of greater literacy and numeracy throughout the population, such skills became relatively more common and thus less able to command relatively higher wages. Third, technological change within the service industries meant that workers could sometimes find themselves and their skills replaced by machines; the ability of the Victorian male clerk to write copperplate lost most of its value with the arrival of 'lady typewriters', as the earliest typists were called, while after the First World War the army of Victorian domestic servants was ultimately routed by gas and electric ovens, washing machines, sewing machines, and the Hoover.

What can we infer about their skills and lifestyles from the differentials in favour of service workers? It is likely that such workers were as well, or better, trained than workers in industry. They almost certainly had to be; service jobs required workers to be literate and numerate. As with most generalizations, there is an exception: the lower ranks of domestic servants, but it serves for the majority. While it was still possible, in the 1880s, for an illiterate man, James Archdale, to found and run a successful engineering business, literacy was a prerequisite of work as a clerk or shop worker or for entry into the old and new professions.

Many service trades, particularly those in transport and communications, required workers to use expensive and complex equipment such as railway engines, telegraphs, or medical machinery, rudimentary as the latter seems by modern standards. Although, as with industrial equipment, much of the training took place on the job, learning by watching, it took a long time;

a main-line railway driver would be unlikely to achieve that position until his mid-twenties, at least five years after achieving full physical strength and having worked his way through posts as a cleaner, fireman, and on shunting and goods engines.[6] Shop-work had less rigid structures, but it is clear from accounts of the foundation of the great grocery chains that extensive experience was needed before a son or (rarely) daughter of the house was trusted in control of a new branch; literacy and numeracy, with a good deal of commercial acumen, were essential.[7]

Service jobs which required work with large amounts of capital equipment tended to be concentrated in large firms; indeed, the capital requirements, particularly in transport and communications, were such that the firms were among the biggest in the country. As already noted, the largest of all, and a byword for secure and well-paid employment among the lower middle class, was the General Post Office, with 212,310 employees in 1907; the next largest, the London and North West Railway, had 77,662. Two-thirds of those employed in the fifty largest British companies were in firms which provided transport or other services.[8] Such large firms required good management and it is no surprise that it was the North Eastern Railway Company who in 1897 introduced a graduate trainee scheme.[9] The infant London School of Economics became heavily involved in running courses for railway staff, establishing a railway department with the support of the companies in 1904; the companies were soon in conflict with Sidney Webb, a founder of LSE, over his support for trade unions and a threat of the removal of their grant of £1,000 to the railway department was enough to secure Webb's removal from the Chair of the Board of Governors. Banks and insurance companies were also becoming large employers of clerical staff, at this time still largely male; in Liverpool in 1871 the twelve marine insurance firms employed 450 clerks and apprentices, an average of nearly 40 clerks per firm, while the Mersey Docks and Harbour Board had 300 clerks and apprentices by 1875.[10]

Training for the professions was much more extensive, and took longer, than for management posts in industry. In most white-collar occupations, new recruits served as apprentices or junior clerks, usually badly paid and overworked; in the North and South Wales Bank, the average apprenticeship lasted five years, for which period the apprentice was paid £80.[11] Even when the status of a full clerk had been attained, promotion came slowly and there were very few positions of real trust and responsibility, such as that of the 'correspondence clerk'. In banking and insurance, it was customary for clerks to move from branch to branch to gain experience and promotion. After perhaps twelve years with the company, an employee could normally expect to become at least a branch manager. Job security was taken for granted in such firms and the few who lost their jobs were guilty of some form of indiscretion. Even in firms without branches, where promotion was more difficult, the clerk could expect steady increases in pay; only in exceptional times, as with the employees of Baring's Bank after the 'Baring Crisis' in 1890–91, were salaries ever cut.[12] But this was most unusual, for the banking system in Britain was very stable, with failing banks quickly replaced by others; the major changes before 1914 aided that stability by the amalgamation of many small banks into the so-called 'clearing banks' which have dominated British banking in the twentieth century.[13]

As the century progressed, more and more professions developed their own qualifications, sometimes tested by written examinations, and their own methods of regulation and forms of association; twenty-one were so regulated in 1880, but another twenty-one had been formed by 1900 and a further twenty-seven by the end of the First World War.[14] Among the earliest to claim professional status were the accountants, with professional bodies established in Glasgow in 1854 and in London in 1875.[15] While some, such as the ancient clerical, medical, and legal professions, came to depend on qualifications gained through formal education, the majority based entry upon experience on the job, what would now be called the 'recognition of competence'. This, and sometimes limitations on the numbers who might be admitted, served as effective barriers to entrance, preserving the exclusivity and thus the value of the service which was performed.

Service workers had thus to be well educated and trained; they earned high wages and salaries and they were, as a consequence, well respected. Such jobs were highly desired, the acme of ambition for the sons of the aspirant working class, not only because of the salaries but also because of the security which went with them; white-collar workers were far less likely to become unemployed and far more likely to spend many years with their firms, even retiring with a pension, a rarity for even the most skilled of manual workers. As a result, competition for white-collar jobs was fierce and employers could afford to be choosy. In 1900 the Great Western Railway administered written examinations for appointment to its salaried staff but, at the same time, took note of the candidate's 'appearance and manner of address' and with this evidence 'weeded out a number of unsuitable candidates who otherwise, if they made a sufficient number of marks, would be accepted'.[16] In many firms, it was almost impossible for an outsider to be employed; posts were filled by recommendation and introduction, often through the influence of friends or family.

Although the lifestyle of the clerk was sometimes a subject of ridicule, as with the ineffable Mr Pooter of George and Weedon Grossmith's *Diary of a Nobody*, it reflected a value to economy and society which was based upon education, training, and scarcity. The same was true of those in the learned professions, who gained in status during the century. While an eighteenth-century aristocrat would treat the doctor, lawyer, or surveyor as a servant, by the mid-Victorian period, these professionals had gained much greater respectability and independent status, earning fees rather than wages. Sir Abraham Haphazard, the lawyer in Trollope's *The Warden*, published in 1858, was a grandee.

There remained, of course, many service industries which did not attain such ranking in the eyes of society and where exploitation and misery were rife, as in other industries. Hotel and catering workers were one such group, while *The Ragged Trousered Philanthropists* attests to the low wages and even the danger, from lead-poisoning or from poor scaffolding, of the life of the painter and decorator. For every Thomas Lipton, founder of the great grocery chain, whose status enabled him to entertain King Edward VII on his yacht, there were thousands of small shopkeepers who struggled to eke out a living on the margins of working-class society.

Domestic servants were on average worse paid, and lower in status, than other workers in services. But the average concealed great variety, from the steward, butler or housekeeper in a large aristocratic household to the 'maid-of-all-work' who was the only servant in a lower-middle-class home. In a large house, servants might have little or no contact with the master or mistress, living in a world 'below stairs' that was governed by its own rules and rituals and knowing their place in a complex hierarchy. *Beeton's Penny Guide to Domestic Service* in the 1880s listed thirteen categories of male and ten of female servants.[17] By contrast, in a small house, living-in domestic servants might suffer from their propinquity to master and mistress; this could produce a clash of class mores and manners which only too often ended in tears, particularly where the mistress struggled, at the expense of maid or cook, to keep up appearances.

The impact of services

As with so many features of Victorian and Edwardian economy and society, the impact which the growth of services had on the family or individual depended to a great extent on their place in the distribution of income and wealth. C. H. Feinstein has estimated that in 1900 consumers spent 21.2 per cent of their overall expenditure on services, but this was an average of the middle and upper earners, at about one-third, and the working classes at less than 10 per cent. As a result, about three-quarters of total expenditure on services was made by the middle and upper earners; they spent most on domestic service (23 per cent), followed by motor cars and other travel (17 per cent), entertainment and betting (9 per cent), and medical services (8 per cent). The working classes, on the other hand, spent most on railways and trams (40 per cent), followed by medical services (16 per cent), life assurance and funeral expenses (11 per cent), and entertainment and betting (10 per cent). (There was also, for all classes, a large residual component which included expenditure on charities, education, hairdressing, and religion.) No comparable figures exist for the middle of the nineteenth century, but it seems likely, on the basis of employment in the service industries, that relatively less was then spent by all classes on travel and entertainment, and relatively more, exclusively by the middle and upper classes, on domestic service.

What benefit came from this expenditure, and particularly from the major expenditures on travel, medicine, and entertainment? What were the results, also, of the growth of retail and wholesale trade?

Travel

For the working classes, travel was throughout the period principally for work. Although leisure travel did expand, with omnibus and charabanc outings and the annual trip to the seaside, it was dwarfed by the morning and evening, and often also lunchtime, journey to and from the workplace. Transport history in the nineteenth century is dominated by the railway, but by the end of the century it is likely that trams and buses provided more journeys. For the upper and middle classes, leisure travel was always more important, although middle-class journeys to work also expanded with the move to suburbia and the building of the suburban railways; by the end of the nineteenth century the network of routes around London and the South-East was, as it remains, the largest and busiest rail commuter network in the world. But travel to seaside resorts or spas, by horse-drawn coach before the coming of the railway, had been important since the beginning of the century, while the 'season' enjoyed by the upper classes had for long involved an elaborate movement between the great houses in London and the country.

In the later part of the century, the taste for the Scottish Highlands, partly established by the royal family, led to a further seasonal migration to shoot grouse or deer. Increasingly, foreign travel, once the preserve of the rich making the Grand Tour, became affordable because of the work of Thomas Cook and his competitors and attractive as some of its dangers were removed. Guidebooks were written and the vogue for wildness, pioneered by the Romantics, spread into a liking for mountaineering, walking, and, late in the century, skiing.

Travel thus became for the upper classes an important part of what Thorstein Veblen described as 'conspicuous consumption'. That is, not only did it give satisfaction to the consumer but it also conferred or confirmed social status. Since travel was by definition undertaken outside the home, it was obvious; moreover, it could be surrounded by a panoply of fashion, in the clothes that were worn or the new technology that was used. Riding in 'The Row' in London's Hyde Park gave opportunities for display of the latest style, as did the plethora of different types of carriages listed in a catalogue for 1883, among them the Victoria Phaeton, the Mail Phaeton, the Four Wheel Dog Cart, the Light Wagonette, the Brougham, the Parisian Phaeton, and the Stanhope Phaeton. Even the technology of the bicycle, relatively cheap as it was, changed rapidly, through improvements to the frame, the tyres, gears, and brakes, as did clothing for cycling. All gave unlimited opportunities for purchase and display.

The most extreme example, however, is the motor car. Early cars were very expensive; the 8,000 new cars purchased in 1900 cost an average of £385,[18] about ten times the yearly wage of an agricultural worker.[19] They were also noisy and, to the irritation of many observers, demanded the transformation of large parts of the country through the building or improvement of roads. In 1909 Charles Masterman protested, in *The Condition of England*, against the 'Wandering machines, travelling with an incredible rate of speed, [which] scramble and smash and shriek along all the rural ways . . .', while *The Economist* argued at the same time against public expenditure on road improvements: 'Here public expenditure is calmly suggested in order to please the richest class of pleasure seekers.'[20] Little good did the protests do.

Medicine

In the twentieth century, expenditure on the 'health-care indus-try' has risen enormously in all the developed countries and now accounts for between 10 and 15 per cent of total expenditure. In Britain in 1900, from the gross national product of £1,926 mil-lion, only £35 million or 1.8 per cent was spent on medical services, two-thirds of it by the middle and upper classes. What did they get for their money?

In simple terms, they got the medical professions and the drugs which doctors, dentists, and nurses prescribed or adminis-tered. The 1901 census recorded 22,486 physicians and surgeons in Britain and 5,149 dentists (who, with an estimated income of £630 per annum, were slightly better paid than doctors with £620). The beginnings of later growth can be seen in the fact that twenty years before there had been only 15,091 doctors and 3,538 dentists; the numbers of both thus more than doubled between 1881 and 1911.[21] Much more numerous, but much less well paid were the 76,067 nurses and 4,123 midwives recorded in the 1901 census, who received about £80 per year including their board and lodging, if they worked in hospitals, and the 5,094 ancillary staff. Total expenditure on medical staff and hospitals was about £25 million. Last, there were pharmaceutical drugs, at an estimated value of £10 million.[22]

This was the great age of patent medicine, in which large fortunes were made from sales of drugs and potions buttressed by extensive expenditure on advertising. Thomas Holloway, later to give his name to Royal Holloway College in the Univer-sity of London, was a merchant in the City when he was given a formula for an ointment by an Italian client; securing a recom-mendation from a surgeon at St Bartholomew's Hospital, he advertised widely, prospered, and, when he died in 1883, was able to leave over £1 million to charity. Jesse Boot began as a shopkeeper making proprietary medicines in 1874 and, by ad-vertising, in 1877 increased his takings by five times; by 1901 he had 251 shops, now also selling stationery and fancy goods, with 560 by 1914. Less respectable, perhaps, was Thomas Beecham, who began as a peddler of patent medicines, herbalist, animal healer, and astrologer, and whose 'Beecham's pills' were the foundation of the family fortune which supported his famous son, one of Britain's greatest orchestral conductors.[23]

A more interesting question, and one which has given rise to heated controversy among historians, is what good this expenditure did to people's health. As described in Chapter 3, the death rate for the whole population began to fall in the 1860s, after a period of stability from the 1830s, although it was not until the early 1900s that infant mortality showed a significant fall. But it is very difficult to know how much of this, or of the simultaneous reduction in illness which is assumed to have occurred, is due to the medical professions or to drugs.

According to the distinguished medical historian, Thomas McKeown, the likely answer is that, before 1935, and certainly in the nineteenth century by comparison with improvements in nutrition, the work of the medical and pharmaceutical professions through therapy and immunisation made little difference to the decline in death rates. It is true that 'from the second half of the nineteenth century a substantial reduction of mortality from intestinal infections followed the introduction of hygienic measures—purification of water, efficient sewage disposal and improved food hygiene, particularly in respect of milk.' The medical profession played some part, of course, in securing these improvements in public hygiene, but otherwise they had little role in reducing mortality. McKeown was not concerned with reductions in non-fatal illness; some drug therapies did make a difference to syphilis, diphtheria, diarrhoeal diseases, and some surgical conditions, but recent studies have shown that little could be done for most chronic conditions from hernia to heart disease.[24]

Other historians believe that McKeown overstated his case, in particular by underestimating the impact of public health measures, but few quarrel with his conclusions about medical treatment. It was palliative in some cases, neutral in others—recall Florence Nightingale's Hippocratic ambition 'to do the sick no harm'—actively harmful in a few, while it remained true that it

was best, if at all possible, to avoid admittance to hospital. This
the middle and upper classes usually managed to do, even to the
extent of having their appendix removed on the kitchen table,
since rates of mortality mainly from cross-infection in the voluntary hospitals and infirmaries were frightening; the introduction
after 1875 of separate wards or hospitals, the 'Fever Hospitals',
did however help to limit the spread of infections. It had earlier
been assumed that patients with infectious and non-infectious
diseases could be mixed in the ratio of one to six, and in 1854 St
Bartholomew's in the City of London still admitted cholera
patients to the general wards.[25]

Doctors, of course, contributed by their own observations and
by scientific study to our better understanding of the causes of
infection, particularly by the water-borne diseases, and thus to
the public health measures which were introduced. They, and
health visitors and nurses, also tried to stem the tide of infant
mortality by emphasizing the benefits of breast feeding, although this was a losing battle against fashion and the spread of
condensed milk. But it is difficult to do other than conclude that
increasing expenditure on individual medical services brought
little benefit to Victorian and Edwardian populations.

Entertainment

One of many images of Victorian society is of the family gathered around the fireside, singing popular songs, reading aloud or
playing word or card games. The image is attested to by many
literary examples and there is no reason to doubt its truth, but it
would be a mistake to see such behaviour as divorced in some
way from the economy, since Victorian and Edwardian enter-
tainments were increasingly provided by or were dependent
upon a growing part of the service sector.

Take family sing-songs. While traditional folk songs may have
continued to be sung, they were rapidly being supplanted by the
supply of sheet music from commercial publishers. The popularity of certain songs depended to a large extent on their performance in music halls or theatres, whose number greatly increased;
in 1868 there were 39 of them in London, 339 in the country as

a whole.[26] The demand for popular music was such that a 'pirate' music publishing business developed in the 1880s and 1890s, successful songs being transcribed on their early public perform-ance and rapidly printed for sale. Despite this, legitimate sales of popular songs were enormous; 'The Lost Chord' sold 500,000 copies between 1877 and 1902, 'In the Gloaming' sold 140,000 copies in the 1880s, and 'The Holy City' sold 50,000 a year in the 1890s.[27] Such semi-religious works were paralleled by substantial sales of sacred music; earlier, Novello and Co. published Handel's *Messiah* in 1848 and by 1849 had sold 20,000 copies. By the 1880s, the same firm's catalogues contained 10,550 separate octavo works and 10,236 in ordinary music size, and 7,000 more titles were published in the 1890s.[28] No wonder that there are said to have been 80,000 pictorial sheet music covers published in the Victorian period.[29]

Home music making depended on there being at least one musical instrument in the home, probably a piano, and on the skills of members of the family. Sales of pianos, pianolas, and other mechanical musical instruments rose rapidly; Ehrlich, the economic historian of the piano, estimates that by 1910 there were 'some two to four million pianos in Britain—say one in-strument for every ten to twenty people' and British makers competed hotly in home and foreign markets with German and American producers. Possession of a piano was an important signal of respectability and the ability to play was an essential attribute of a young lady, despite the view of the *British Medical Journal* in 1892 that 'the chloroses and neuroses from which so many young girls suffer' were the result of piano practice; poor piano playing had, in the view of the Editor, 'driven studious men from their books to the bottle . . . and stimulated peaceable citizens to the commission of violent assaults.'[30] Small wonder that there was a growing demand for music teaching and that the number of 'Musicians and Music Masters' rose from 26,000 in 1881 to 47,000 in 1911.[31]

As popular literacy increased, so did sales of newspapers and books. By 1900 consumers were spending £14.9 million per annum on these forms of entertainment and expenditure was rising rapidly, increasing by 55 per cent even by 1913.[32] The circulation of the popular press was very large, while on the eve of the First World War *The Times* sold 45,000 copies daily and the *Morning Post* about 150,000. Among the popular papers, the *Daily Mail* is said to have had 1 million readers by 1900.[33]

Thus entertainment within the home became increasingly commercialized. Outside the home, the same was true for both spectator sports and leisure. Among soccer teams, Charlton Athletic began as a boys' club, playing in an old quarry, Sheffield United were a works team, and Wolverhampton Wanderers began as St Luke's Church Football Club; cricket teams remained divided into 'Gentlemen' (the amateurs) and 'Players' (the professionals), but soccer rapidly became a professional or semi-professional sport. The demands of spectators of these and other sports, and the intervention of private promoters, led to extensive investment across the country in football, cricket, rugby, and other grounds and pitches. Often, these were combined with public parks, a form of Victorian municipal enterprise which did something, at least, to soften the rigours of urbanization; sport was encouraged also as an alternative to crime. The most popular teams needed their own grounds, to house large and growing Saturday crowds; attendance at the FA Cup Final rose from 6,000 in 1880 to 73,833 in 1899, and even county cricket matches could attract over 50,000 spectators.[34] The increasing professionalism of sport demanded clear sporting rules; most were codified in the period between 1860 and 1900, when sport became an important British export. Cricket and polo spread across the Empire, but football followed trade and colonized the whole world.

Closely allied to sport was betting. Informal working-class gambling was widespread early in the nineteenth century, on dog-fighting, cock-fighting, rabbit coursing, pigeon shooting, ratting and pitch-and-toss. In the second half of the century, however, the invention of the telegraph facilitated mass gambling on horse-racing, despite the legal prohibition on off-course betting. Betting took place in pubs and working-men's clubs, in factories, yards, and mills, and the 'bookies' runner' was a familiar figure.

By 1869 twenty sporting newspapers were published in London alone.

Capital and revenue expenditure on leisure within existing towns was probably surpassed, however, by the costs of building and running the new holiday and retirement towns. These were principally seaside resorts, modelled on the Prince Regent's beloved Brighton, designed to extend the opportunity of seaside holidays, or at least days at the seaside, first to the middle and then to the working classes. Many were both holiday resorts and places to which the Victorian middle classes retired. Although the development of the large retirement communities such as Peacehaven and Rottingdean had to wait until the years after the First World War, by 1911 all the leading resorts had a high proportion of retired or unoccupied men in their populations.[35] These developments not only enriched a number of landowners who were prescient enough to develop their estates but then provided livelihoods for the myriad of hotel-keepers, landladies and shopkeepers who catered to the residents and the holiday trade. Bournemouth, for example, did not exist in 1838, but by 1911 it had over 78,000 inhabitants. Established and guided by an alliance of landowners and the local council, it began with the building of large villas but from the 1870s, with the opening of a branch railway, became a popular summer and winter resort.[36]

Retailing and wholesaling

Travel, entertainment, and medicine are all services which can readily be described and, at least roughly, measured. Much more difficult to describe, because of its great variety, or to measure, because it cannot always easily be distinguished from production or manufacture, is the whole complex of distribution services which we call retailing and wholesaling.

By 1914, Britain had developed department stores, chain stores and the Co-op to add to the high street and village shops; it was by then unusual to buy direct from the manufacturer or food producer, although milk would still be delivered by a local dairy and bread purchased from the neighbourhood baker. Expensive items might still be ordered 'made to measure', for example from the tailors or couturiers who provided the clothes of the upper classes, but most goods came in standard sizes and uniform packaging had largely replaced the paper bags or packages in which groceries such as tea, coffee or sugar had hitherto been weighed and sold. London emporia such as Selfridges and Harrods or their equivalent in provincial towns had been built to attract the 'carriage trade', while, at the other end of the retail spectrum, Thomas Lipton and his competitors fought for the patronage of the working man and woman, on the basis of large volumes, small margins, and tied suppliers. Advertising, another growing service industry, was crucial in the success of such retail chains.

In 1830, few of these types of retailing had existed. Shopkeeping still had some of the dubious reputation which it had attracted in the Middle Ages and the early modern period, born of a suspicion of the middleman who would inflate prices, withhold goods from market or adulterate quality. The latter charge, that of adding chalk to flour, watering the beer or, much worse, adding various poisonous substances to food, was substantiated in accounts of retailing for the poor. As a result of a lengthy investigation by *The Lancet* into the adulteration of milk, conducted from 1851 to 1854, legislation was passed in a rather weak Act of 1860, nevertheless the first in what was to become a typical Victorian moral crusade for food purity. By the end of the 1880s bread, beer, and tea were free from adulteration, but milk still caused concern. On average, it contained 25 per cent of water, added after one-third of the cream had been skimmed. To avoid a watery appearance, dairymen added 'flour or starch . . . to thicken its consistency, the juice of boiled carrots to give a "fullness and sweetness", chalk for whiteness and even brains to froth the milk'.[37] About half the milk sold was chemically dyed. Despite successive legislation and inspection, adulteration continued into the twentieth century, although on a reduced scale.

The crusade against adulteration was one of the reasons for the development of the Co-operative Movement. The first Co-op was founded by the 'Rochdale Pioneers' in 1844 as a deliberate attempt to provide a quality service to the poorer sections of the community. Others followed and by 1900 there were 1,439 societies with a combined membership of 1.7 million, while a wholesale department was founded in 1855. The Co-op captured, for the poor, the economies of bulk purchasing which they could not, individually, secure. It provided an alternative to the corner shop which, however well located and friendly, could often lead the poor housewife into debt by the provision of credit.[38] Once in debt, she was unable to complain about poor quality.

There had, however, already been substantial changes before 1830 from a pre-industrial pattern of retailing. The great fairs, an important means of selling goods in medieval and early modern Britain, had largely disappeared, although a few specializing in livestock survived, and local markets were declining in importance, losing their place to fewer and larger wholesale markets. Some itinerant salesmen survived, for example in the drapery trade, as the descendants of the medieval peddlers, but they were a vanishing breed. In the nineteenth century, very large shops emerged; the drapers James and William Campbell of Glasgow had a turnover of over £1 million in 1850 and employed about 300 people, while in London at the same time Shoolbred and Co. of Tottenham Court Road was the largest retail drapery firm in the country, with over 500 employees and a turnover of at least £1 million. Some pioneers of the ready-made clothing trade were of a similar size.[39] Plate-glass and gas lamps adorned these shops, which based their success on three innovations: no credit, fixed and marked prices for cash sales, and small margins achieved on a high volume of sales. All three contributed to higher labour productivity and to lower prices. They were so successful that some observers questioned whether the small shop could survive, a question that has been asked ever since!

An important retail service was that concerned with death. The high mortality of the Victorian period, together with the elaborate funeral and mourning rituals, provided a consistently high demand for a variety of services. As early as 1841, Jay's 'Mourning Warehouse' was established in Regent Street in London, providing a range of mourning cards, stationery, and the crêpe ribbons which were, for much of the late nineteenth century, an important product of the textile industry.[40] At least among the middle classes, strict adherence to mourning clothes was essential: 'For brothers and sisters, six months was sufficient: three in crepe, two in black and one in half-mourning' (subdued colours). Jet jewellery was essential during mourning, supplemented by rings, brooches, and bracelets made from the hair of the dead relation. Funerals ranged in cost in 1874 from £10–£15 for a tradesman to £500–£1,500 for the wealthy.

The history of retailing has not been adequately told, but even less is known about the wholesalers, both those who supplied the retail shops of Britain and those who imported and exported much of the enormous foreign trade of the country. In some cases, as with the large drapers, wholesale and retail trade was merged, but there were also many merchants who never dealt direct with the ultimate customer. The task which they faced in coping with the growth of the British population and its relocation into the great cities was considerable. The coming of the railways, which permitted physical distance between producer and consumer, was a particularly important influence on the developing wholesale trade in food; one benefit was an increasing degree of 'quality control'. The introduction of branded goods and packaging followed. But the organizational task was immense, particularly in dealing with perishable goods like milk, which had to be delivered in small quantities to millions of customers.[41]

Both retailing and wholesaling were intensely competitive industries with high labour productivity. Successful retailers, particularly those catering for working-class clients, seem to have become so by a policy of cutting margins, specializing in only a few products and seeking reliable sources of supply, often from overseas. Thomas Lipton, for example, called his early shops 'Irish markets', emphasizing that they sold ham, butter, and eggs from Ireland; in 1877–8 he issued his own 'Lipton Pound Note', promising for 15 shillings (75p) as much of these products as would cost £1 elsewhere. To cope with the resulting demand his main Glasgow market in 1878 had a horseshoe counter 100 feet long. No credit was given and no deliveries made, in a sharp contrast to more traditional grocers.[42]

The middle and upper classes continued, however, to demand high quality service. In London in 1887, William Whiteley, 'The Universal Provider', as he styled himself, boasted that he could supply 'anything from a pin to an elephant', delivered by his 320 horses and 145 vehicles. By the end of the century, the major London stores had branched out into mail order, with the 'Army and Navy Stores' making a speciality of the supply of the Empire; their catalogues are a compendium of Victorian consumption. They offered, for example, 40 varieties of briar pipes and 13 different types of lavatory paper. Harrods, who were the first to take orders by telephone, summed up their service in their telegraph address: 'EVERYTHING, LONDON'.

It seems certain that such competitive pressures as the 'ruthless war' between Lipton and other shopkeepers, concentrating on the staple products of the working-class diet, produced lower prices for consumers. Advertising might seem to add to their costs, but was justified by higher volume sales, serviced by well-trained staff, efficient bookkeeping, and good stock control. British retailing's success in the twentieth century was based on good foundations in the nineteenth. Together with the other service industries, it made a major contribution to economic growth and to improving living standards.

10

THE OPEN ECONOMY

Free trade, fair trade, and the Empire

Far more than the Factory Acts, the introduction of state schools or even 'The Irish Question', free trade was the most hotly debated and most divisive political issue of the 'long' nineteenth century which ended with the First World War. It split the Conservative Party in the 1840s and came near to doing so again sixty years later. It divided industrialists from City financiers and was greatly affected by attitudes to the growth of the Empire and the emergence of the Commonwealth. Even in the 1990s it lives on in attitudes to the European Union.

It is therefore surprising that economists and historians have agreed for some time that the sweeping reduction of tariffs on imports in the 1840s, and even the abolition of the Corn Laws which was pushed through Parliament by Sir Robert Peel in 1846, had little overall effect on the growth of the British economy. It can even be shown that foreign trade as a whole was of much less importance to the British economy than is often assumed and that British living standards in, say, 1900 would only have been marginally lower if Britain had not traded at all.[1]

Imagining Britain in the late nineteenth century without exports of cotton goods and without imports of wheat may seem so far from reality as to have no purpose. But it helps to make the point, first made in the 1770s by Adam Smith, that exporting goods has no purpose in itself; just as we sell our own labour, we export to enable us to buy the things that we want and cannot efficiently make or grow for ourselves. In a very small number of cases, it would be impossible to produce some commodity in Britain but, in most cases, we import goods not because we could not make them but because it is (perhaps only slightly) cheaper for us to get them overseas and (perhaps only slightly) cheaper for the foreign producer to buy what he wants from us. This is the basis of the economist's principle that it is 'comparative advantage' which underlies and produces trade; each person and each country plays to its relative strengths and gets the benefits of specialization. In doing so, as Ricardo demonstrated in 1817, we all become richer.[2]

Why, then, was there so much fuss about free trade? Partly, it is because politicians and others think in terms of national rivalries, with trade as a symbol or symptom of victory or defeat. Thackeray was moved by the display of artefacts in the Crystal Palace in 1851 to write:

> These England's triumphs are
> The trophies of her bloodless war.[3]

But the real answer, as with so much else in economic history, lies in the distribution of the income from that bloodless war. Tariff and trade policy, or any other form of intervention by government in the economy, alters the relative income or wealth of different groups within society. Unless the policy is catastrophic in its consequences, it is unlikely greatly to affect the overall output of the economy, but it can produce wealth or poverty for particular people, who naturally have a strong view on what the policy should be. Trade policy is therefore a central feature of the theoretical and practical debates which make up what is known now, as in the eighteenth and nineteenth centuries, as 'political economy'.

Free trade—winners and losers

The debate was first given intellectual coherence and vigour in the 1770s with Adam Smith's attack on the mercantilist thought and economic policy which had dominated British economic and trade policy since the seventeenth century. The principal object of mercantilism was to increase British wealth; this was not equivalent to the modern objective of economic growth, but was instead defined as the accumulation of assets in or owned by Britain. In modern terminology, this could be achieved by maximizing a positive balance of payments, increasing exports and reducing imports so as to increase British ownership of assets. This can be caricatured as a desire to build up larger and larger stocks of gold, the medium of international exchange and payments at that time, but it was really a desire to build up productive and trading capacity in Britain and to inhibit production of competing goods overseas.

Mercantilist policy was enshrined in a multitude of statutes which, even after they were rationalized or repealed in the 1820s, imposed over 2,000 duties, on almost every conceivable commodity, although only 17 of the 721 protected articles produced 94.5 per cent of the total tariff revenue in 1840.[4] In addition to tariffs on imports, there were bounties for exports, particularly of grain, while the Navigation Acts exercised tight controls on the British colonies, ensuring that most colonial produce was channelled through Britain and carried in British and colonial ships. There was even, until 1824, a prohibition on the emigration of men with engineering and mechanical skills, while the export of machinery was prohibited until 1842, although the controls were widely evaded. Not all tariffs were designed primarily to inhibit imports; in a country such as Britain in the eighteenth century, with a relatively primitive structure of government and civil service, it is easier to secure tax revenue through indirect taxes such as customs duties than by direct taxes such as the income tax. Although an income tax was imposed briefly during the Napoleonic Wars, it was repealed when peace returned and tariffs, together with excise duties principally on the production of alcohol, were then again, until the 1840s, the main method of financing government.

The intellectual case against tariffs was stated by Adam Smith in the 1770s and elaborated by David Ricardo in his *Principles* in 1817. This settled the argument for most economists, but although the tariff structure was greatly simplified by Huskisson in the 1820s, its major features remained unchanged. One tariff in particular, the Corn Laws, became the focus of such political and popular discontent that it spawned the Anti-Corn Law League, dedicated to its abolition; the results, including a split in the Conservative Party and the eventual abolition of the Laws in 1846, were described above in Chapter 6.

Despite this political upheaval, the history of British agriculture in the next twenty years, described in Chapter 6, shows that Corn Law repeal did not justify at the time either the hopes of its advocates or the fears of its opponents. There were no immediate winners or losers, except Peel himself. This was partly because the Corn Laws had not actually increased grain prices in all years before 1846, partly because their abolition did not cause prices to fall. The explanation of this paradox is that British agriculture had been successful in increasing the production of grain and other foodstuffs in the years after 1815, so that grain prices had rarely reached levels at which the Corn Laws could be invoked to allow imports; when they did reach such levels, the poor suffered through real wages which may have been as much as 12 per cent lower than they would otherwise have been.[5] After 1846, however, at least for fifteen or twenty years, the pressure of rising populations and rising incomes in Britain and throughout Europe (from which most grain imports would have had to come) led to rising prices which both protected farmers from the predicted ruin and disappointed the hopes of the working classes and manufacturers alike.

Winners and losers began to appear in the 1860s. The planting of the prairies in Canada and the United States then combined with the expansion of Russian and German grain exports to supply the growing British markets at lower and lower prices; Russia supplied almost as much wheat to Britain as the United States in the 1860s, remained the second largest source and surpassed the United States for much of the period from 1904 to the First World War.[6] The results of Britain's adherence, throughout this period, to free trade while other European countries retained or renewed protection can be seen in the fact that British bread prices were much lower and that British grain production was much smaller.

This was unambiguously good for British consumers. But it should not be assumed, despite their protests, that it was unambiguously bad for British farmers and landowners. As was explained in Chapter 6, their reaction was to specialize in other products, in particular those such as liquid milk, vegetables, and fruit, which were naturally shielded from foreign competition because of difficulties of preservation, transport or storage. The transition to new products was, as it usually is, an uncomfortable one but it did not permanently impoverish British farmers, as some had feared. It certainly diminished at least for a time the incomes of British landowners and aristocrats, who were forced in many cases to reduce rents as their tenants struggled, but this was a redistributive effect which, many would argue, was long overdue.

Assessing the other winners and losers from Britain's move to free trade is made difficult by the fact that, although most other countries in the world economy followed, or were pressurized by Britain into emulating, the British move, most of them soon retracted. The fifteen or so years after the Cobden–Chevalier Treaty of 1860 with France was the period when the world economy came closest to accepting free trade, but the United States remained protectionist throughout and it was only the Dutch and Danes who continued to share Britain's policies while other European nations returned to protection. Thus the question is not: 'who benefited from a world of free trade?', to which at least the theoretical answer is: 'everyone'. Rather, it is: 'who gained and who lost in an increasingly messy world of protection, often ingeniously disguised in a multitude of regulations?'

By the end of the nineteenth century, many of the manufacturers whose fathers and grandfathers had welcomed the end of protection in the 1840s were no longer so sure. Free trade was clearly of benefit to British industry when it reduced the prices of imported raw materials and gave free access for British goods to overseas markets where there were no foreign competitors.

While that was so, British firms could effectively act as oligopolists (few sellers faced with many buyers), and reap the rewards of being first in the field. But such advantages rapidly diminished, both because other British and foreign firms were quick to enter the competition and because, after the 1870s, foreign governments increasingly protected their home industries. Cries of 'unfair competition' began to rend the air.

In those circumstances, many industrialists were attracted to the Tariff Reform campaign launched in 1903 by Joseph Chamberlain; so too were the advocates of the interests of the Commonwealth and Empire, arguing for 'Imperial preference' for imports from those countries. Both arguments were decisively rejected at the General Election of 1906, probably in the main because of the spectre of higher food prices. But given the dominance of Britain in world trade at the time, despite its adherence to free trade, voters were almost certainly right both for themselves as consumers and for the country as a whole to prefer freedom to buy in the cheapest markets to the introduction of subsidies to British industry at the expense of British consumers.

This was principally because British trade, unlike the trade of most countries before 1914, was so large and so important to the workings of the world economy that its direction and development had significant effects on the economies of other countries. Essentially, Britain used its exports of manufactured or part-manufactured goods—35 per cent of world trade in manufactures by 1914—and of services such as banking and shipping to buy foodstuffs and raw materials from the under-developed world and to buy manufactures from the United States and the rest of Europe. With the income from those sales, Americans and Europeans could then join Britain in buying from the rest of the world. The result was more and more rapid investment in the developing world and, overall, the faster growth of world incomes than would have been the case if Britain had re-adopted protection. Thus, although Britain could have done without trade, it is a good thing for the world economy that it did not.

Foreign investment—winners and losers

By the middle of the nineteenth century 'the City', the collective term for the bankers, financiers, and traders gathered in London and particularly in the Square Mile of the ancient Roman capital, was convinced that its future lay in free trade and in freedom to invest overseas. It had also persuaded itself, as is natural with most interest groups, that what was good for the City was good for Britain. By and large, these attitudes have remained ever since. Did Britain, or other sections of British society, really win or lose from the activities of the City before 1914?

The question is important because a central, though by no means the only, activity of the City was that of directing British funds overseas at a rate which has not been matched before or since by Britain or any other country. By 1913, 32 per cent of Britain's net wealth was invested overseas, as a result of annual flows of foreign investment which built up from 1–1.5 per cent of gross national product before 1850 to 2.1 per cent in the 1850s, 2.8 per cent in the 1860s and 4.3 per cent in the whole period from 1870 to 1914.[7] In other words, for much of the late nineteenth century about one-twentieth of everything earned by Britons was used to buy assets abroad and, by the time of the First World War, one-third of everything owned by Britons was in a foreign country. Needless to say, these averages conceal the fact that almost all the assets were owned by an élite section of the British population. Many of them, or their fathers, grandfathers, or friends were in the City and the growth of overseas assets was the City's work.

The simplest test of whether this investment policy was sensible for these rich individuals is to ask whether they could have invested their money more profitably elsewhere. The answer seems to be that they could not have done so. There were two possible alternatives to what actually occurred: the first was to invest the money within Britain and the second was to invest it overseas but in a different way. Studies of the returns which were achieved by matched investments in Britain and overseas have concluded that, on average, more money could be made by investing overseas, although there were distinct cycles when, in turn, one type of investment was better than another.[8] The gap in returns did not stem from greater risk in foreign investment, but probably from the greater opportunities in opening up new worlds.

It is more difficult to know whether investors should have pursued different investments overseas. This was an exceptional period not only in the sheer volume of overseas lending and purchases but in the way in which it was done. Investors from other countries, principally Germany, France, and the United States, at this time, and British investors before the 1850s and after 1919, did pursue different strategies; they either invested heavily in direct purchases of land, buildings or businesses in foreign countries, or they bought bonds issued by foreign governments. British investors between 1850 and 1914, by contrast, put probably at least 70 to 80 per cent of their money into what is called 'portfolio' investment; they bought shares or bonds in private companies trading overseas. This strategy strongly suggests that British investors were relatively 'risk-averse', that is, they did not want to put all their eggs in one basket, or even a few, baskets, but preferred to spread their money around, to minimize the overall risk if a single investment failed. It is difficult to argue that they were wrong in the volatile conditions of the time; some might have made more money on a few well-judged direct investments or by purchasing bonds from countries which continued to pay the interest, but the volume of investment was such that it is difficult to believe that all could have done so.

This conclusion, that the City got it right for itself and its investors, is not very surprising. It is because the City has usually got it right that London remains one of the three financial centres of the world and that the British upper, and to some extent middle, classes are as wealthy as they are; this is true today and it was self-evidently true in 1914, when the City was unrivalled.

But simple questions are not always the most interesting ones. Even if the City acted in its own and its investors' interests, it is still possible that its investment criteria were wrong or that a different investment strategy could have brought greater benefits to the British economy. The City has certainly been accused, in the nineteenth century and ever since, of neglecting possibilities for investment in domestic British industry, of discriminating against small and medium-sized businesses in Britain, and of insisting on rapid returns to investment which preclude long-term projects to build industrial capacity. Some historians have even ascribed the relative decline of the British economy after 1919 to poor investment strategies before 1914. It is argued that the City should have stimulated and funded the development of new, technologically advanced, industries which would have replaced the old British staple industries of coal, iron, steel, cotton, and shipbuilding. They did not do so and thus won, by their short-term criteria, while the British economy lost.

The simplest version of this charge, as expressed in modern headline terms, is that the City was 'exporting jobs', in other words that the money could have been used within Britain to create employment for British workers. There are two difficulties with such an attack. First, although there were short-term peaks in unemployment (during the cycles discussed in Chapter 1), there is no evidence of structural unemployment or underemployment of the labour force between 1830 and 1914 of the kind that was to afflict Britain in the 1920s and 1930s, so there was not much scope for job-creating investment. Second, there is no evidence that British industrialists had difficulty in raising funds, by borrowing or issuing shares, when they wished to do so; many did not, preferring to generate investment funds from their own profits, but it is difficult to blame the City for not responding to a demand which did not exist.

More fundamentally, British overseas investment did create 'British jobs' in two senses; first, much of the investment, for example in railway building, produced flows of orders for equipment made in Britain. Second, much of the investment helped to reduce the cost of food in Britain and thus left more of British incomes to be spent on manufactures or services, with consequent benefits to workers in those fields.

Before 1914, it is very difficult to show that British investors took a short-term view. Most foreign investments were in long-term projects like ports, railways, and land clearance, and investors were content to wait, sometimes many years, to achieve returns. It may be that Britain should have modernized its industries and developed many new ones before 1914 but the fault, if there was one, does not seem to lie with the City. It certainly won, but the British economy did not thereby lose.

The Empire—winners and losers

The Empire 'on which the sun never sets' was not only—or perhaps even primarily—created to make money. The motives of soldiers, settlers, missionaries, merchants, and traders and of the British government itself were always mixed. Many economists and politicians, particularly in the eighteenth and early nineteenth century, were convinced that it was a mistake to acquire colonies; they were difficult to administer, expensive to pacify and defend, and conferred only doubtful benefits in giving access to raw materials. The revolt of the American colonies at the end of the eighteenth century only confirmed this view, although the British West Indian colonies continued for some time to provide income for plantation owners like Sir Thomas Bertram in Jane Austen's *Mansfield Park*. There was little sense of opportunities for economic development, with Australia seen as fit only to dump criminals and most of Africa thought to be unsuitable for white settlement. Only India, the jewel in the crown, was different.

During the nineteenth century, the bounds of the Empire became 'wider still and wider'. In 1830, it consisted essentially of Canada, Australia, New Zealand, Sierra Leone, the West Indies, the Cape Colony, Burma, and, with varying degrees of formal and informal control, India. Singapore, Malta, Gibraltar, and Hong Kong became important naval stations. The period of greatest expansion was between 1860 and 1910, principally in Africa with the acquisition of what was to become South Africa, Rhodesia, Nyasaland, Nigeria, Gambia, the Gold Coast, the

Sudan, and Egypt, effectively annexed in 1914. In Asia Malaya was added and British Guiana became the only formal British possession in Latin America.

Since at least the end of the nineteenth century, there has been argument about the origin of the Empire. Not only because motives changed in two centuries, with different people at different times influencing its course, but also because so much of its creation was opportunistic, there is no single cause or simple explanations. Among those who provided partial answers are Hobson and Lenin, who—though differing in detail—saw imperialism as a stage of economic development and the Empire as an outlet for surplus funds created by capitalism; those historians who have seen the Empire as a vehicle for British trade; and those who see in the 'scramble for Africa' an extension overseas of European power conflicts. The most recent theory, put forward by the historians Cain and Hopkins, is that the Empire was the creation of 'gentlemanly capitalism', an aspect of the supremacy of Britain within the financial services industries centred in the City of London.

But for whatever motives, the Empire was created and by 1914 Britain controlled 25 per cent of the land mass of the world, the largest Empire in human history. By 1911, 22 per cent of British exports went to, and 37 per cent of British imports came from, that Empire. Between 1853 and 1910, 1.5 million English, Welsh, and Scots had emigrated to Canada and 1.3 million to Australia and New Zealand.[9] They and their descendants in the countries of white settlement, Canada, Australia, New Zealand, and South Africa now numbered over 15 million. They were soon to repay their debt to the 'mother country' by sacrificing 225,000 men and £4.5 billion in the European war.[10] Is it conceivable that the Empire was, in economic terms, a mistake for the country as a whole, even if many British individuals either at home or in the colonies made their fortunes from it?

The simple answer is that there was not much in it; Michael Edelstein has put it graphically by pointing out that the Empire in 1914 was probably less important to British economic growth than the railway had been in 1860 and that either could have been dispensed with at that stage of their development at the cost of less than five years of economic growth.[11] This may seem extraordinary, but it stems from a careful consideration both of the costs of Empire and of the benefits which it conferred. It is crucial to remember, in making such calculations, that the countries of the Empire would not have disappeared off the face of the globe if they had not been colonized. They might, in the absence of the British, have developed as independent nations or, perhaps more likely, they would have been colonized by someone else.

If the former, they would no doubt, like every other country in the world, have turned to Britain to buy manufactures and to be a market for their food and raw materials. Britain could then have traded with them without all the bother of governing them. If the latter, then it is possible to imagine a scenario in which France, Germany, Belgium, Spain, Portugal, Italy, or the Netherlands—the other colonial powers—annexed the land and refused to allow British migrants to settle or anyone to trade with Britain. But this is unlikely. None of these colonial powers refused to trade themselves with Britain, although they did erect tariff barriers to try to protect some of their home industries from the inroads of British goods. There is no reason to believe that they would have been more protective of their new, hypothetical, colonies. In other words, the world economy, as distinct from the world coloured red on the Mercator projection, would not have looked very different.

Such excursions into 'counterfactual' or hypothetical history are fascinating and illuminating but can easily become too far divorced from reality as ramification succeeds complication. It is clear that the private as opposed to the social gains to imperialism were substantial; that is, private individuals made money from the Empire possibly at the cost, or at least without great benefit, to British society as a whole. Some made large sums and established themselves with their wealth in high society, but probably the greatest gainers were the millions of British migrants who voted with their feet to seek a better life overseas. In doing so, they raised the incomes of those who were left and, in many cases, sent money back to those whom they left behind. Many a Scottish croft or English cottage was more comfortable as a result.

11

ECONOMIC RULES

Mandates and meddling

The Victorian and Edwardian period was, as described in Chapter 2, a time of risk. There was risk of death and disease, risk of social disapproval, risk in business or commerce. But there was also approval for those who overcame risk, who fought off the ever-present danger of descent into the abyss of poverty and by their own efforts achieved independence, security, and respect. The immensely popular works of Samuel Smiles, for example, lauded self-help and, through biographies of leading industrialists and engineers, praised those who had succeeded against the odds.[1] Risk-taking itself was praised as a characteristic which set such men apart from the common herd. It was an essential attribute of the entrepreneur but also of the hundreds and thousands who set themselves up 'in a small way of business' in the hope of betterment.

Such vocal admiration of risk-taking in Victorian and Edwardian society is paradoxical, however, because it went hand-in-hand with a gradual reduction in the individual's freedom to take risks. All economic life depends on the existence of a set of rules of behaviour, implicit or explicit, codified or embodied in precedent, upon which men and women can base their expectations and their decisions. But the rules cannot be so rigid that they stifle initiative and innovation. Just as the rules of many sports were codified in Britain between 1830 and 1914, so rules were made and, often after heated public debate, remade, which set the conditions for economic development and for individual economic achievement.

It is likely, in fact, that the setting of rules was the main contribution of nineteenth-century governments to economic life. At least by twentieth-century standards, the direct expenditure of government, financed by taxation, was low except in time of war; neither state spending nor the complex set of transfer payments which today characterizes the welfare state were a significant feature of the nineteenth century. One major exception was the Poor Law, while there were stirrings of the growth of the state in expenditure on education, law and order, and transport, for example through mail contracts to shipping lines. But there was no direct spending on subsidies to industry or agriculture, nothing on individual and little on public health. The government took no responsibility for fostering economic growth, although it gradually began to attempt to smooth out economic fluctuations through the operations of the independent Bank of England.

Throughout the nineteenth century, therefore, government expenditure remained a much smaller proportion of national income than has become the case in the late twentieth century, when levels of 40 to 50 per cent (including transfer payments such as unemployment benefit) are not uncommon. Expenditure was high at the start of the century as the enormous loans raised to pay for the Napoleonic Wars were serviced and repaid, but by 1831 expenditure had fallen to 16 per cent of GNP, the highest figure for the rest of the century. In 1870 and 1890 it was as low as 9 per cent and, for most of the time, was not more than £3.5 per head per annum.[2] The central government bureaucracy or civil service also remained small. There were 25,000 civil servants working for central government in 1815 and only 39,000 in 1851, 54,000 in 1871, and 79,000 in 1891.[3]

In these respects, therefore, British governments of the nineteenth century appeared to follow John Stuart Mill's maxim that 'the business of life is better performed when those who have an immediate interest in it are left to take their own course, uncontrolled either by the mandate of the law or by the meddling of any public functionary.'[4] In other fundamental ways, however, Mill's maxim was ignored; by 1913, the mandate of the law extended over wide areas of personal and economic life, even if the 'age of free trade' had reduced the impact of government in other ways. To enforce such laws there were school inspectors, railway and factory inspectors, customs and excise officers, and police. Meanwhile, local government assumed more and more powers and responsibilities. The 1911 Census recorded 321,000 public functionaries, central and local, against the 43,000 of 1841.[5] But, even so, the direct influence of government was less than its indirect effect through the rules which it set or which evolved by the decisions of the courts.

Outrage and evidence

How and why did the rules change? The antecedents of much nineteenth-century legislation can be traced in an invaluable treasure trove for historians, the 'Parliamentary Papers' or 'Blue Books'; these record in many folio volumes, published each year throughout the period, the results of the thoughts, research, evidence, and statistical investigations of a multitude of politicians, lobbyists, reformers, and interest groups. The modern British institution of parliamentary questions to ministers, by which Members of Parliament seek to elicit information or make political points, grew only gradually in the nineteenth century, though 4,824 were asked in 1897 and 7,705 in 1914;[6] nor was there an equivalent of the permanent select committees which now, however inadequately, monitor the work of individual government departments. Without these institutions, MPs were able to harry ministers mainly by 'moving for' papers or for the setting up of a select committee which would look into the issue in question. In addition, government also found it convenient, perhaps as a delaying tactic but often as a genuine attempt to gather evidence and form policy, to establish a Royal Commission of investigation. The papers produced and the minutes of evidence and reports of committees and commissions, together with the annual reports of various public officials, form the Parliamentary Papers.

The period from 1830 to 1914 is punctuated, in fact, by Committees and Commissions which attained fame for their careful investigation and the influence which their reports had. But why was a Committee or Commission established in the first place and why did new laws result? One theory is that the enquiries were a response to public outrage, forcing itself on a rather unwilling state. Checkland, for example, argued that British governments, by contrast to those of much of continental Europe, had no paternalistic tradition which would lead them to intervene in the economy or to right social wrongs. Nor did they have any experience of regulating industries or the growing cities. Lacking a systematic view of society, governments therefore did not have a coherent economic or social policy; in fact they had a positive bias against such policies. Instead 'each specific situation had to reach such a level of deterioration as to be an outrage against public opinion. Secondly, the indifference and hostility that stood in the way of remedy had to be in some manner and to some degree weakened. Thirdly, the forces pressing for improvement had to attain such strength as to be effective.'[7] In other words, governments acted when public scandal was so great that they could not remain inactive. A good example is that of legislation against child prostitution stimulated by the investigations of W. T. Stead in 1885 when he published 'The Maiden Tribute of Modern Babylon' in the *Pall Mall Gazette.*

An alternative view is that social and economic laws were attempts by the government, on behalf of the upper and middle classes, to exert control over the working classes by formal means, buttressed by the power of the state; this was intended to complement the less formal social controls which stemmed from deference, the influence of religion, and the accepted rules of social behaviour. Thus nineteenth-century governments came to control public order and private morality by legislation, among much else, to establish police forces (1835), to censor plays (1843), to control the licensing of pubs (1872 and 1904), to punish homosexuals (1885), to ban gambling except on racecourses (1845), cock-fighting (1849), bear-baiting (1835) and bare-knuckle fighting (from 1835),—though never fox hunting, the pleasure of the landed classes—to raise the age of sexual consent for girls to 16 (1885), to license cinemas (1909), and, for a time, to seek to register prostitutes through the Contagious Diseases Acts (1864, 1866, and 1869). These increased and sometimes hotly contested controls over public and private behaviour were balanced, on this theory, by giving the working classes an increasing degree of political power through the extension of the franchise.

A third view ascribes a great deal to a few men and even fewer women. Much nineteenth-century legislation and executive action by governments can be traced to the actions of a few influential and hard-working people who harangued, badgered, and persuaded their colleagues. Edwin Chadwick (1800–90), for example, was immensely influential in the administration of the Poor Law, in enquiries into sanitary conditions, in the establishment of registration of births, marriages and deaths, and in enforcing competitive examinations for jobs in the Civil Service. John Simon (1816–1904), a surgeon, began his career in public health when he became medical officer to the City of London in 1848. He became Medical Officer to the Privy Council in 1858 and to the Local Government Board in 1876 and was an indefatigable, if often cantankerous, campaigner for improvements to public health. Joseph Bazalgette (1816–91), an engineer, became Engineer to the Metropolitan Commission of Sewers in 1852. He created the Embankment to the Thames and built a network of sewers. Thomas Barnardo (1845–1905) devoted himself to the care of homeless and destitute children and is estimated, by his death, to have helped 250,000 children through the organizations which he founded. Later, Sidney Webb (1859–1947), originally a barrister, became with his wife, Beatrice, the dominant social campaigners of the early twentieth century. All these and many others can claim credit for the social legislation of the period.

No single theory can easily explain the plethora of legislation. Some 'moral panics', such as the campaign against the use of arsenic in wallpapers and foodstuffs, did not lead to legislation despite a fervent press campaign; but greater awareness of the dangers and consumer pressures led to a decline in its use.[8] Each

Act represented victory for a particular interest group, its views often moderated by the objections or amendments of opponents and occasionally overturned by changes in public opinion or the demonstration that the legislation had not worked. The Contagious Diseases Acts, for example, were repealed after a successful campaign against the discrimination implied in trying to control venereal disease only through controls on women. But the vast majority of laws remained on the statute book. What difference did they make?

Rules and their economic effects

Perhaps the most fundamental of economic rules are those concerned with the ownership and transfer of what English law knows as 'real property' and Americans as 'realty', in other words land and buildings. Perhaps 90 per cent of the population in the nineteenth century had the resources only to occupy, rather than own, land or houses and most did so only on weekly tenancies; they could be evicted at the will of the landlord at the end of each week.[9] But for the small proportion of the population who had sufficient resources to buy or lease, it was of great importance to have legal proof of their ownership and an economical and efficient means of buying and selling; this was particularly so since investment in houses was one of the major forms of saving undertaken by the middle classes. As a result, by the end of the century urban property was held on leasehold or through tenancies 'in small parcels by a multitude of small and medium-scale owners', although the great bulk of rural land and of urban freeholds remained in the hands of the wealthy.[10] As Offer summarizes the pattern: 0.86 per cent of proprietors owned 30 per cent of the land by value and 'More than a million house proprietors coexisted in the shade of a few thousand landowners with very large concentrations of tenure.'[11]

It was unfortunate, for all these landowners and landholders, that Parliament proved unable, for almost the whole of the period, to legislate for the transfer of property in ways that met the needs of buyers and sellers. Instead, it set rules which benefited the legal profession, most of whose income came from conveyancing, the transfer of property. The Law of Property, Offer concludes, was a 'vested interest of the legal profession. . . . a species of corporate property'.[12] The foundations of this property were the failure, because of resistance from the lawyers, to institute a registry which could hold details of each property and its owner or tenant, while the monopoly was further guarded by arcane documentation and a body of legal precedent which was so complex that most lawyers could not understand it. As a result, searches for proof of ownership had to be undertaken over and over again as property was sold and resold, and the slightest error could give rise to juicy fees. The 'rent' on the property, arising from the monopoly position of lawyers, was substantial; in 1898, for example, property worth £393 million was transferred and about 2 per cent of that sum was paid to solicitors—the branch of the legal profession whose bread-and-butter work it was.[13] Small wonder that, in the nineteenth century as in the twentieth, the number of lawyers grew much more rapidly than did the population as a whole. By 1901 there were 16,000 solicitors in England and Wales.

It was not that this professional monopoly was unexamined. There were in fact four Royal Commissions on the costs of land transfer between 1830 and 1870 and one failed attempt in 1862 to establish a Land Registry in London. After 1870, the pressures for land reform in Ireland and Scotland and the views of Radicals who saw land registry as a prerequisite to a redistribution of property ensured that the issue became a major source of party political debate. Lawyers employed every trick to delay, obfuscate or render meaningless any reform that was introduced; as one Lord Chancellor put it in arguing against compulsory registration: 'However stringent you might make the compulsory clause, the ingenuity of conveyancers would be able to defeat it.'[14] It was only in 1881 that payment according to the value of the sale replaced payment by the length of the documents, which had been an encouragement to legal prolixity if ever there was one. Compulsory registration in some parts of the country became a reality only in 1899 and even then the Law

Society, the solicitors' trade union, did not give up; another Royal Commission followed and, in 1922, a Law of Property Act which restored solicitors' incomes while extending compulsory registration. Even today, that process of registration does not yet encompass all property.

This example has been described at length to make the point that rules matter. The rules determined that solicitors should gain from a 'lucrative and largely superfluous function' while property-owners lost.[15] At the same time, other rules instituted in the nineteenth century benefited landowners at the expense of leaseholders, until they were changed by the political pressure for leasehold reform in the late twentieth century. The development of the coal and iron industries was significantly affected, likewise, by the complexities of land ownership which put great power into the hands of landowners, from whom pit-owners had to lease their sites. Meanwhile, the interminable controversies in the late nineteenth century about the rates (local taxation), about taxation of land values, and about the incidence of inheritance taxes, most of which have reverberated ever since, testify to the vital significance which the rules of tenure have for the political and landowning classes and the professions who serve them.

Rules of tenure are fundamental to the operation of an economic system and the nineteenth century merely brought new aspects to the fore. But the technological changes of the period brought the need to make new law to cope with new industries. A prime example is the railways, where Parliament and the legal system groped towards regulation and control of a new technology, seeking to adapt old legal maxims and precedents to a new situation. As with the registration of land, it is difficult to escape from the conclusion that a primary aim, in doing this, was to retain ample opportunities for the payment of lawyers. In the early period of the so-called 'railway mania', as the *Railway Gazette* put it in 1848, the great majority of sham railways had been 'manufactured designedly for fraudulent purposes by lawyers alone', while the conduct of lawyers and judges had created 'a heap of reckless fraud, injustice, misery, ruin and dishonour'.

The procedure for authorizing railway construction was tortu-ous and extremely expensive, but once the railways were built they found themselves enmeshed in new legal issues. Railways were the first of the large employers; disputes soon arose about the extent to which they could be held liable for the actions of a single employee, over whom it might be very difficult for them to exert control. The resolution of such issues demonstrates the extent to which law is the creation of a particular social system. On the one hand, it was held by judges that railway employees (who were mostly drawn from the working classes) had to bear, in return for their pay, all the risks of the job, including that of injury by another worker; on the other hand, passengers (who were mostly from the middle classes) were entitled to claim compensation from the railways for any accidents. The latter judgement gave rise to a vast industry of personal injury litiga-tion. As one historian puts it: 'The range of lucrative opportu-nity that the railway movement presented to English lawyers was staggeringly large.'[16]

Changes in the rules or laws affecting industry and commerce were debated less vigorously than those affecting land or the railways, but were no less significant. There were several financial scandals in the seventeenth and eighteenth centuries such as the 'bubbles' of speculation in the shares of the East India Company and in tulip bulbs. Large fortunes were made and lost, and, in the absence of any public regulation, there was strong public and legal prejudice against any weakening of the rules of liability that made individuals, or their partners in busi-ness, fully responsible for any debts incurred. Unlimited liability and the threat of debtors' prison were considered indispensable deterrents to fraud and incompetence.

During the nineteenth century, however, the rules were gradually changed. Joint-stock companies could at first be formed only by individual Acts of Parliament which could be secured only for enterprises which were so large in scale that they were clearly beyond the capacity of any individual or part-nership to undertake; the great trading companies such as the East India Company, the turnpike trusts which built roads in the eighteenth century and finally the canal and railway companies benefited from this exception. The last also gained, again by the Acts which instituted them, privileges of compulsory land purchase, although they paid through regulation and price controls for their special quasi-monopoly status. From 1825 onwards this status could be more easily gained, but still only for the very large undertakings.

Industrial and commercial enterprises in general, however, remained subject to unlimited liability. This was workable and equitable for small businesses, in which each partner could be expected to know the business and to keep an eye on the others, but it did not work well when businesses grew so large that such day-to-day control was impossible or when the need for investment in machinery or buildings outran the capacity of the partners to finance it. Then outside capital was required and, although for a time loans on the security of a mortgage might provide, by the middle of the nineteenth century the pressure for means of raising funds persuaded Parliament, in the Companies Acts of 1855 and 1862, to allow the formation of limited liability companies; this was despite continued popular suspicion, shown in the epithet given by *The Times* to the 1855 Act: 'The Rogues' Charter'.[17] Businesses were in fact slow to take advantage of the new freedom, probably because the owners and their families were loath to cede control to outside shareholders.

The increased freedoms and privileges granted, often after prolonged campaigns of lobbying, were inadequately matched by Companies Acts which began to prescribe methods of accounting and auditing. Owners who had been used to treating their firms as their private property found it difficult to keep their hands out of the till; managing directors were aghast when shareholders objected to their 'borrowing' from the business. It was to take some generations before custom and practice accorded with legislative intentions.

The freedom of industry to operate as it wished was also increasingly circumscribed by legislation to promote safety and to protect workers and customers. The *laissez-faire* doctrine, that a bargain made between employer and employee should not be interfered with, was first breached in the case of women and children; such weak creatures, it was argued, could not adequately protect themselves and so the state must intervene to do so. It took decades before the protection was adequate, but the process really began with the Factory Act of 1833, both because it was the forerunner of later legislation covering many different industries and, most importantly, because it established an inspectorate. Although their powers with respect to individual employers were initially limited, and local magistrates were slow to punish even flagrant breaches of the rules, the inspectors had an invaluable tool in publicity and in their right to report to Parliament and thus to the public. It was through those reports, published in the Parliamentary Papers and summarized in the press, that working conditions in factories and mines were brought to general attention, the first step towards regulation; the inspectors ranged widely, for example by measuring the heights and weights of factory children and comparing them with other groups, by describing occupational diseases and the dangers of machinery, and by drawing attention to the dangers of chemical pollution to the public.

The first effective Factory Act, that of 1833, seems to twentieth-century eyes to be amazingly permissive. It covered only the textile trades and limited the work of children under 13 only to an eight-hour day, to which two hours of compulsory school was added, and of adolescents under 18 to eleven hours, although the inspectors could also regulate the ventilation and temperature of the buildings in which the children worked. But the extent of control was gradually increased in 1847, 1851, and 1853, and broadened in 1842 and 1850 to cover the mines; in both cases, the initial protection of children soon extended to women. There remained, of course, many industries outside textiles and mining in which there was neither control nor inspection, but in which enquiries, such as the Children's Employment Commission of the 1860s, revealed equally appalling working conditions. It was only in 1864 and 1867 that legislation stopped the cleaning of chimneys by young children climbing up or down them, only in 1873 that the employment of children under the age of eight on farms was prohibited. Controls were gradually extended to cover most industries in the 1870s and 1880s. Wages, as distinct from conditions, were left to the market; only in 1909, after decades of agitation about the 'sweated trades', were Trade Boards established to provide machinery for setting wages in tailoring, shirt-making, and confectionery.

The move to more rules sounds, in these terms, as if it was smooth and progressive. It was not; each piece of legislation was hotly contested and its passage accompanied by baleful predictions of ruin for the industries affected. In some cases, these fears were shared by the advocates of change, but it was argued that the evils, revealed for example by the *Report of the Commission on the Employment of Women and Children in Mines and Collieries* (1842), were so terrible that they must be stopped at whatever cost. It took many years for the consciousness of changing technology to convince employers that there were other, and possibly even more profitable, ways of working which did not involve maiming young children. Indeed, arguments that further regulation of the working hours of children would make British industry uncompetitive are still heard in the 1990s from opponents of the social chapter of the Maastricht Treaty.

The hand of the state

In some areas of the economy, the state did more than make the rules. Nationalized industries, despite Conservative propaganda to the contrary, were not an invention of Labour governments in the 1940s. The Royal dockyards, ordnance factories, and the mint had been part of the public sector, to use twentieth-century terminology, since the Middle Ages. The Royal Mail had been a public corporation since the reign of Charles I, but it was not until the 1830s that governments saw the post as a public service rather than a source of revenue. The penny post and its accompanying stamps were the recognition of this and the precursor of an enormous expansion of the Post Office, such that by 1914 it was by far the largest employer in Britain and had moved into other fields with the creation of the Post Office Savings Bank in

1861 and, from 1912, the establishment of a monopoly over the telephone system.

The most significant act of nationalization in Victorian Britain was, however, the Telegraph Act of 1868, introduced by the Conservative Prime Minister Benjamin Disraeli, which brought into public ownership the various private telegraph companies which had been created since the effective innovation of the technology in the 1840s. Although those companies had been responsible for a rapid increase in telegraph traffic within Britain and its extension overseas with Channel and transatlantic cables in 1851 and 1866 and many overland cables—Britain was connected with India in 1864—it was argued that further growth could come only with public control. Most significant in promoting nationalization, however, was the power of the press, which had come increasingly to rely on the telegraph for the transmission of news and which, in the early 1860s, resented the imposition of increased charges. The *Quarterly Review* had asked in 1854: 'Is not telegraphic communication as much a function of government as the conveyance of letters?',[18] so that the success of the Post Office as a public corporation encouraged the state to foster the age of communication. Public pleasure at the penny post was a powerful argument.

The principle could, of course, be extended to other economic activity and there was serious thought, for example, of the nationalization of the railways. In the event, the power of the railway companies and their shareholders staved off state ownership, but from the 1840s the quasi-monopoly of the railways and their impact on the economy and on the urban and rural landscape ensured that they were subject to state control unlike that on any other industry. Acts of 1842, 1844, and 1846 set up inspectorates, controlled profits and enforced the running of the cheap 'Parliamentary Trains', while control over fares and safety continued throughout the century. In other forms of public transport, municipal enterprise extended without difficulty to local buses and trams. The principle of the regulation of monopolies led, also, to the control of gas and electricity prices and, ultimately, to the control of these industries by the local authorities.

Substantial as these extensions of public ownership and control were, they were essentially marginal to the lives of most of those who lived in Victorian and Edwardian Britain. It is doubtful whether most of the population knew or cared that their tram was owned by the local council or their telegraph office by the government. But one form of state intervention, the Poor Law, was central or significant to the lives of several millions. It was certainly not new, for relief and control of the poor had been a major concern of government since medieval times, but the title 'The New Poor Law of 1834' is given to the legislation which ruled government poor relief until after the First World War.

The Act of 1834 sought to systematize poor relief on the basis of utilitarian principles and at the same time to limit the growth in expenditure on the poor which had frightened the middle classes, who paid for it, since the Napoleonic Wars. In its purest form, rarely if ever attained in practice, it limited relief to the poor who were willing, or were forced, to enter workhouses; there they were subjected to a regime deliberately designed to be 'less eligible', in other words even more miserable, than the life which they had led in the community. The Boards of Guardians, middle-class members of the local communities who were appointed to administer the Poor Law, gradually established workhouses for this purpose from the 1830s onward; they sought simultaneously to limit 'out-relief', the payment of money to the poor in their own homes. Except in times of great distress, help was rarely given to able-bodied males, so that the bulk of recipients of poor relief—like the bulk of the poor—who were subjected to this increasingly severe regime, were the young, the old and the sick.

From the 1870s onwards the 'crusade against out-relief' had as its particular targets two groups among the poor, the elderly and widows with children; their self-reliance, reformers urged at the time, was being sapped by indiscriminate charity. Partly as a result, the numbers in the workhouses rose steadily. In the early 1870s, for example, 11 per cent of males and 8 per cent of females over sixty-five in London were in the workhouse, where even elderly husbands and wives were separated, and by 1905–9 these proportions had risen to 18 per cent and 9 per cent respectively; the proportions in the rest of the country were consistently lower but nevertheless reached, by 1905–9, 7 per cent of males and 3 per cent of females in the north of England and 5 per cent of males and 2 per cent of females in the south.[19] By the early twentieth century, it is true, the worst rigours of the workhouse regime were being relaxed for children and the elderly, but the workhouse retained its stigma and, as MacKinnon puts it, 'only the poorest of the poor' were likely to enter it.[20] But, as out-relief declined from the position in the early 1870s when 3.5 per cent of the population received it on any one day, to the situation in the 1890s, when less than 2 per cent did so, they had little alternative.[21]

It was only with the welfare reforms of the Liberal governments between 1906 and 1914 that poor relief began to change, while at the same time the state came more actively to intervene in social policy. The introduction, at least for some parts of the working class, of old age pensions in 1909 and health insurance and unemployment benefits in 1913, had only a small effect before the First World War. However, because the two latter schemes were contributory they began the process of removing the stigma of charity from the relief of poverty; they substituted instead the concept of payment in time of distress as a right, bought by contributions in better times. Even if the motives of politicians in promoting the legislation owed as much to fears of physical deterioration among the working class—fuelled by alarmist reports of the heights and weights of recruits to the armies which fought the South African War—as to a desire to remove the shame of poverty, these laws began the process which led ultimately to the welfare state.

Conclusion

In 1831 the great historian Lord Macaulay reflected that, by contrast to the men and women of his own age, in the eighteenth century: 'They knew luxury; they knew beggary; but they never knew comfort.' By 1914 the comfort which, even in Macaulay's day, had been the preserve only of a small part of the population, had spread to the majority. By their efforts, building on the inheritance of the early years of industrialization, the average man, woman, or child was much richer, the range of goods and services which they made, bought, and enjoyed much wider.

These men and women, of all classes, occupations, and parts of the British Isles had also created the political, military, and economic power which allowed the citizens of some small islands off the coast of Europe to control by 1914 the greatest Empire which the world has ever seen. This control was based on the invention and successful exploitation of many new technologies and on the creation and command of unprecedented financial resources. These inventions and investments depended on the ingenuity and skills of a population which had turned, earlier than any other people in the world, from agriculture and commerce to manufacturing, trade, and services.

It was certainly an extraordinary period in the history of the British Isles. It is no surprise that the achievement still exercises a strong hold over the British imagination, as it did at the apogee of Empire in 1902. Then, to celebrate the Coronation of Edward VII, was first sung 'Land of Hope and Glory'. Ever since, however, millions have participated in a collective act of memorial to that lost age when:

> Wider still, and wider, shall thy bounds be set.
> God, who made thee mighty, make thee mightier yet.

and when 'Victorian Values' were a reality rather than a slogan for politicians bemoaning the loss of a golden age. That loss was soon to come for the Edwardians, as Rudyard Kipling predicted it would when he wrote in *Recessional* that:

> Lo, all our pomp of yesterday
> Is one with Nineveh and Tyre

both on the battlefields of the First World War and, later, with the loss of Empire after 1945.

To invest Victorian and Edwardian Britain with a golden glow is misleading. To do so is, first, to ignore the reality of economy and society, of the life of the people, which this book has sought to depict. It was certainly a period of growth, of change, of improvement in the human condition, a time when the bulk of the British population escaped through effort and ingenuity from the malnutrition, illness and misery which had been the lot of most people in the eighteenth and early nineteenth centuries, as in all previous centuries. Despite the cycles of boom and depression which disfigured the period, Victorian and Edwardian Britain saw the creation of a consumer society, based upon the invention and innovation of a myriad of 'things' and the provision of a myriad of services beyond the imagination of earlier generations. As the society grew richer, it was able better to care for all its members, even if some of the 'Victorian Values' of charity, independence, and self-help could sometimes turn into a punitive attitude to those who failed.

It was an age, of course, in which luxury and beggary continued to coexist with comfort. Most of the comfortable middle class which came to power in the late nineteenth century was still prepared, in the name of individual liberty, to tolerate extremes of poverty, pockets of misery, exploitation, and despair, which even those who unthinkingly extol Victorian values would not wish to see again. But they tempered individualism with a sense of community and an acceptance of the need for communal action to improve society and to regulate the economy.

Many lasting monuments, streets, schools, universities, town halls, museums, concert halls, still bear witness to that action and to those beliefs. It was in many ways a spectacular time.

But the myth of the golden Victorian and Edwardian years can also be misleading, even dangerously so, if it is allied to a denigration of the British economy and society in the twentieth century. It leads then to a search for scapegoats who can be blamed for the apparent fall from the high peaks of Britain's imperial glory. It is important to remember that, however substantial the achievements of the period from 1830 to 1914, Britain's economic growth in the twentieth century has been faster and greater. At the same time, British society has become more civilized, more tolerant, and more equal than it was at any time in the Victorian or Edwardian age. Some of the foundations of those changes were laid before 1914, in the protection of the workers through the Factory Acts, in the Liberal welfare reforms, in the growth of trade unions, and in the foundation of the Labour Party which was ultimately to bring the Welfare State to Britain. Nearly one hundred years later, we are still benefiting from the work which was begun then. Such a development would have surprised but also pleased many of the men and women who strove, in the Victorian and Edwardian age, for social improvement and for economic opportunity for all the people. This, rather than imperial triumphalism, is what we should celebrate when we think of this remarkable age.

NOTES

Introduction (pages 1–2)

1. Adam Smith, *The Wealth of Nations* (1776), 625.

Chapter 1 (pages 3–21)

1. P. Johnson (ed.), *20th Century Britain: Economic, Social and Cultural Change* (Harlow, 1994). The average annual wage in 1913 prices was £69 in 1913–14 and £370 in 1991.
2. F. Capie and G. Wood, 'Money in the economy, 1870–1939', in R. C. Floud and D. N. McCloskey (eds.), *The Economic History of Britain since 1700*, 2nd edn. (3 vols., Cambridge, 1994), ii. 220–1.
3. G. Stedman-Jones, *Outcast London* (Oxford, 1971).
4. T. Veblen, *The Theory of the Leisure Class* (London, 1924).
5. Source: R. C. O. Matthews, C. H. Feinstein and J. C. Odling-Smee, *British Economic Growth 1856–1973* (Oxford, 1982), 113, 501.

Chapter 2 (pages 22–40)

1. John Stuart Mill, 'The Spirit of the Age' (1831), in G. L. Williams (ed.), *Mill on Politics and Society* (Hassocks, 1976), 171.
2. B. Seebohm Rowntree, *Poverty: A Study of Town Life* (London, 1901), 86–7.
3. *Life and Labour of the People in London* (London, 1892).
4. M. Anderson, 'The social implications of demographic change' in F. M. L. Thompson, *The Cambridge Social History of Britain, 1750–1950* (3 vols., Cambridge, 1990), ii. 48–50.
5. Calculated from death rates given in B. R. Mitchell, *British Historical Statistics* (Cambridge, 1988), 60–4.
6. Quoted in J. H. Treble, *Urban Poverty in Britain, 1830–1914* (London, 1979), 152.
7. Rowntree, *Poverty*, 135.
8. L. Davidoff, 'The family in Britain', in Thompson, ii. 95.
9. P. Johnson, 'Small debts and economic distress in England and Wales, 1857–1913', *Economic History Review*, 46 (1993), 65–87.
10. A. Briggs, *Victorian Things* (1988), 41.
11. P. Johnson, *Saving and Spending: The Working-Class Economy in Britain, 1870–1939* (Oxford, 1985).
12. Parliamentary Papers, *Report on a General Scheme for Extra Mural Sepulture*, PP 1850, xxi, p. 681.

13. V. A. C. Gatrell and T. B. Hadden, 'Criminal statistics and their interpretation', in E. A. Wrigley, *Nineteenth Century Society: Essays in the Use of Quantitative Methods for the Study of Social Data* (Cambridge, 1972), 368.

14. Briggs, *Victorian Things*, 42.

15. G. Newman, *Bacteriology and the Public Health* (London, 1904), quoted in P. J. Atkins, 'White poison: The social consequences of milk consumption in London, 1850–1939', *Social History of Medicine*, 5 (1992), 217.

16. P. J. Atkins, 'Sophistication detected: Or, the adulteration of the milk supply, 1850–1914', *Social History*, 16 (1991), 338.

17. Quoted in P. W. J. Bartrip, 'How green was my valance? Environmental arsenic poisoning and the Victorian domestic ideal', *English Historical Review*, 109 (1994), 895–9.

18. A. Hardy, 'Rickets and the rest: Child-care, diet and the infectious children's diseases, 1850–1914', *Social History of Medicine*, 5 (1992), 397–8.

19. Information in this paragraph from calculations by Anderson, 'Social Implications', 21–3.

20. Briggs, *Victorian Things*, 106, 189, 206, 209.

21. J. Benson, *Coalminers in the Nineteenth Century* (Dublin, 1980), quoted in R. A. Church, *The History of the British Coal Industry: 1830–1913: Victorian Pre-eminence* (Oxford, 1986), 584.

22. L. Leneman, 'Lives and limbs: Company records as a source for the history of industrial injuries', *Social History of Medicine*, 6 (1993), 405–28.

23. Dr William Sharp, quoted in R. Gray, 'Medical men, industrial labour and the state in Britain, 1830–1850', *Social History*, 16 (1991), 28.

24. Ibid. 32.

25. H. Southall and E. Garrett, 'Morbidity and mortality among early nineteenth century Engineering Workers', *Social History of Medicine*, 4 (1991), 237–9.

26. Estimate given in Matthews *et al.*, *British Economic Growth*, 75–6. No source is given.

27. Quoted in R. C. Floud, K. W. Wachter and A. Gregory, *Height, Health and History: Nutritional Status in the United Kingdom, 1750–1980* (Cambridge, 1992), 56–7.

28. A. Redford, *Manchester Merchants and Foreign Trade* (2 vols., Manchester, 1956), vol. ii, p. xxii, quoted in R. A. Church, *The Great Victorian Boom, 1850–1873* (London, 1975), 53.

29. Source: calculated from Mitchell, *British Historical Statistics*, 695.

30. Source: calculated from R. C. Floud, *The British Machine Tool Industry to 1914* (Cambridge, 1976), 39.
31. Quoted in Briggs, *Victorian Things*, 40.
32. B. S. Supple, *The Royal Exchange Assurance: A History of British Insurance 1720–1970* (Cambridge, 1970), 109.
33. Private information on modern rates from Mr Jim Elsey of London Guildhall University.
34. Supple, *Royal Exchange Assurance*, 116.
35. J. Frome Wilkinson, *The Friendly Society Movement* (1886), 204, quoted in Johnson, *Saving and Spending*, 65.
36. P. H. J. H. Gosden, *The Friendly Societies of Britain, 1815–1875* (Manchester, 1961), quoted in G. Best, *Mid-Victorian Britain, 1851–70* (London, 1979).
37. C. Chinn, *Better Betting with a Decent Feller: Bookmaking, Betting and the British Working Class, 1750–1990* (New York, 1991).
38. Davidoff, 'The family in Britain', 114.

Chapter 3 (pages 41–56)

1. R. C. Floud *et al.*, *Height, Health and History*.
2. J. C. Riley, *Sickness, Recovery and Death: A History and Forecast of Ill-Health* (London, 1989), 171.
3. Southall and Garrett, 'Morbidity and Mortality', 231–53.
4. S. Szreter, 'The importance of social intervention in Britain's mortality decline *c.*1850–1914: A reinterpretation of the role of public health', *Social History of Medicine*, 1 (1988), 1–38, but see also S. Guha, 'The importance of social intervention in England's mortality decline: The evidence reviewed', *Social History of Medicine*, 7 (1994), 89–114.
5. D. E. Baines, 'Population, migration and regional development', in Floud and McCloskey, *Economic History of Britain*, vol. ii, table 13.1.
6. D. E. Baines, *Migration in a Mature Economy: Emigration and Internal Migration in England and Wales 1861–1900* (Cambridge, 1985), 282.

Chapter 4 (pages 57–75)

1. Source: Mitchell, *British Historical Statistics*, 389–90.
2. Source: C. H. Feinstein, *National Income, Expenditure and Output of the United Kingdom, 1855–1965* (Cambridge, 1972). T85 for capital expenditure, T61 for consumers' expenditure.
3. M. J. Daunton, *Housing the Workers* (London, 1990), 207, 214.

4. D. J. Rowe, 'The North East', in Thompson, *Cambridge Social History*, i. 438.

5. D. J. Olsen, *The Growth of Victorian London* (Harmondsworth, 1979), 213.

6. L. Davidoff and C. Hall, *Family Fortunes: Men and Women of the English Middle Class, 1780–1850* (London, 1992).

7. R. McKibbin, *The Ideologies of Class: Social Relations in Britain 1880–1950* (Oxford, 1990), 143.

8. A. Huxley, *An Illustrated History of Gardening* (London, 1978), 295.

9. Ibid. 281–4.

10. Source: Mitchell, *British Historical Statistics*, 259; J. Langton and R. J. Morris, *Atlas of Industrialising Britain, 1780–1914* (London, 1986), 164–6.

11. Sir Edwin Chadwick, Supplementary report on the Result of a special inquiry into the practice of interment in towns, *Parliamentary Papers* 1843, xii.

12. Parliamentary Papers 1850, *Report on a General Scheme for Extra Mural Sepulture*, PP 1850, xxi, pp. 619–20.

13. Chadwick, *Supplementary report*, 134.

14. Michael Faraday, in a letter to *The Times*, 9 July 1855.

15. Royal Commission, *The Pollution of Rivers* (1867), 38, quoted in B. W. Clapp, *An Environment al History of Britain* (London, 1994), 75.

16. L. Levi, *Wages and Earnings of the Working Classes* (London, 1867), quoted in C. G. Powell, *An Economic History of the British Building Industry, 1815–1979* (London, 1980), 42.

17. Source: Feinstein, *National Income*, T85 and T42.

18. Source: ibid., T42.

19. Powell, *Economic History*, 43.

20. Daunton, *Housing the Workers*, 228.

21. Ibid. 224, including quotation from PP 1843, xxxvi, appendix B.

22. Best, *Mid-Victorian Britain*, 69–70.

23. Ibid. 42.

24. M. E. Falkus, 'The British Gas Industry before 1850', *Economic History Review*, 20: 3 (1967), 499, 503; P. Deane and W. A. Cole, *British Economic Growth: 1688–1959* (Cambridge, 1967), 273.

25. W. H. Preece, 'Recent progress in telephony', *Journal of the Society of Arts*, 30 (1882), 965–9, quoted in B. T. Robson, *Urban Growth: An Approach* (London, 1973), 165.

26. Ibid. 167.

27. P. S. Bagwell, *The Transport Revolution from 1770* (London, 1974), 153–5.

28. R. Millward and S. Sheard, 'Government expenditure on social overheads and the infrastructure in England and Wales, 1870–1914', *University of Manchester Working Papers in Economic and Social History*, 23 (1993), 9.

29. Daunton, *Housing the Workers*, 226–7.

30. C. W. Boyd (ed.), *Mr Chamberlain's Speeches* (London, 1914). The speech, on 'State Socialism and the Moderate Liberals', was given 28 April 1885.

31. G. Sutherland, 'Education' in Thompson, *Cambridge Social History*, iii. 158.

32. *Encyclopaedia Britannica* (London, 1910), 551.

33. C. More, *Skill and the English Working Class, 1870–1914* (London, 1980), 64.

34. Ibid.

35. Matthews *et al.*, *British Economic Growth*, 573.

36. Ibid. 113.

Chapter 5 (pages 76–93)

1. N. J. Smelser, *Social Change in the Industrial Revolution: An Application of Theory to the Lancashire Cotton Industry, 1770–1840* (London, 1959).

2. J. Bourke, 'Housewifery in working-class England, 1860–1914', *Past and Present*, 143 (1994), 167–97.

3. H. Cunningham, 'Leisure and Culture', in Thompson, *Cambridge Social History*, ii. 280–8.

4. Matthews *et al.*, *British Economic Growth*, 69–73, 102–5.

5. D. R. Green, 'Distance to work in Victorian London: A case study of Henry Poole, Bespoke Tailors', *Business History*, 30 (1988), 179–94.

6. M. Barker, 'The middle class journey to work in Newcastle upon Tyne, 1850–1913', *Journal of Transport History*, 12 (1991), 107–34.

7. Olsen, *Growth of Victorian London*, 320.

8. Briggs, *Victorian Things*, 346.

9. Ibid. 335.

10. Ibid. 336.

11. E. H. Hunt, *Regional Wage Variations in Britain, 1850–1914* (Oxford, 1973), 295.

12. Ibid. 326.

13. Ibid. 333.

Chapter 6 (pages 94–109)

1. Mitchell, *British Historical Statistics*, 196, 225, 230.

2. Ibid. 770.

3. Ibid. 722–4.

4. William Cobbett, *Cottage Economy* (London, 1821), quoted in D. J. Oddy, 'Food, drink and nutrition', in Thompson, *Cambridge Social History*, ii. 257.

5. R. B. Weir, 'Brewing and distilling', in Langton and Morris, *Atlas of Industrialising Britain*, 122.

6. J. K. Walton, *Fish and Chips and the British Working Class, 1870–1940* (Leicester, 1992).

7. Oddy, 'Food, drink and nutrition', 266.

8. Ibid. 273.

9. C. O'Grada, 'British agriculture 1860–1914', in Floud and McCloskey, *Economic History of Britain*, vol. ii, table 1.

10. Mitchell, *British Historical Statistics*, 1, 866–7.

11. M. Overton, 'Agriculture', in Langton and Morris, *Atlas of Industrialising Britain*, 34–48.

12. G. R. Boyer and T. J. Hatton, 'Did Joseph Arch raise agricultural wages? Rural trade unions and the labour market in late nineteenth-century England', *Economic History Review*, 47 (1994), 310–34.

13. Food and Agriculture Organisation, 'Energy and protein requirements: report of a joint FAO/WHO/UN expert consultation', Technical Report Series 724 (Geneva, 1985).

14. Royal Commission, *The Employment of Women and Children in Agriculture* (1843), PP 1843, xii, pp. 1–37.

15. P. A. David, *Technical Choice, Innovation and Economic Growth: Essays on American and British Experience in the Nineteenth Century* (Cambridge, 1975).

16. O'Grada, 'British Agriculture'.

17. E. J. T. Collins, 'The age of machinery', in G. E. Mingay, *The Victorian Countryside* (London, 1981), 200–13.

Chapter 7 (pages 110–124)

1. D. J. Jeremy, 'The hundred largest employers in the United Kingdom, in manufacturing and non-manufacturing industries, in 1907, 1935 and 1955', *Business History*, 33 (1991), 94.

2. Ibid. 96.

3. K. Warren, *Armstrongs of Elswick: Growth in Engineering and Armaments to the merger with Vickers* (London, 1989).

4. Floud, *The British Machine Tool Industry*, 40.

5. P. Joyce, 'Work', in Thompson, *Cambridge Social History of Britain*, ii. 157.

6. G. N. von Tunzelmann, *Steam Power and British Industrialization to 1860* (Oxford, 1978), 29–30; J. W. Kanefsky, 'Motive Power in British Industry and the accuracy of the 1870 Factory Return', *Economic History Review*, 32 (1979), 374.

7. I. C. R. Byatt, *The British Electrical Industry, 1875–1914* (Oxford, 1974), 74.

8. N. Rosenberg (ed.), *The American System of Manufactures* (Edinburgh, 1969).

9. E. E. Williams, *Made in Germany* (London, 1896).

Chapter 8 (pages 125–134)

1. Briggs, *Victorian Things*, 54.

2. D. Smith, 'Sir William Bazalgette', *Transactions of the Newcomen Society*, 58 (1986–7), 97.

3. M. Girouard, *The Victorian Country House* (New Haven, 1979), 242, 454.

4. Mitchell, *British Historical Statistics*, 390, 386.

5. Bartrip, 'How green was my valance?', 898.

6. G. Crossick, *An Artisan Elite in Victorian Society: Kentish London 1840–1880* (London, 1978), 76.

7. Mitchell, *British Historical Statistics*, 104.

8. Quoted in F. D. Klingender, edited by A. Elton, *Art and the Industrial Revolution* (London, 1968), 92.

9. Ibid. 94.

10. Ibid. 117.

11. Ibid. 130.

12. Select Committee 1862, *Injury from Noxious Vapours*, PP 1862, xiv, pp. 1, 29.

13. Briggs, *Victorian Things*, 289.

14. Information in this paragraph and succeeding paragraphs is taken from Church, *History of the British Coal Industry*, 17–48.

15. H. S. Jevons, *The British Coal Trade* (London, 1915), quoted in Briggs, *Victorian Things*, 294.

16. Jevons, quoted in Church, *History of the British Coal Industry*, 17.

17. Ibid. 31.

18. Mitchell, *British Historical Statistics*, 247–8 and 252–3.

19. Church, *History of the British Coal Industry*, 780.

20. A. S. Wohl, *Endangered Lives: Public Health in Victorian Britain* (London, 1983), 214, quoted in Church, *History of the British Coal Industry*, 781.

21. Briggs, *Victorian Things*, 317.
22. Church, *History of the British Coal Industry*, 781.
23. C. J. Richardson, *Rus in Urbe: Or Flowers that Thrive in London Gardens or Smoky Towns* (London, 1886).

Chapter 9 (pages 135–157)

1. Smith, *Wealth of Nations*, 430.
2. R. M. Hartwell, 'The service revolution: the growth of services in modern economy 1700–1914', in C. M. Cipolla, *The Industrial Revolution* (London, 1973), 362–3.
3. E. Roberts, *A Woman's Place: An Oral History of Working-class Women, 1890–1940* (Oxford, 1984), quoted in Bourke, 'Housewifery in working-class England', 173.
4. J. G. Williamson, 'The structure of pay in Britain, 1710–1911', *Research in Economic History*, 7 (1982), as reported in Mitchell, *British Historical Statistics*, 153.
5. C. Lee, 'The service industries', in Floud and McCloskey, *Economic History of Britain*, ii. 126–7.
6. More, *Skill and the English Working Class*, 127–8.
7. P. Mathias, *Retailing Revolution: A History of Multiple Retailing in the Food Trades Based upon the Allied Suppliers Group of Companies* (London, 1967), chaps. 3–9.
8. Lee, 'The service industries', 136, quoting Jeremy, 'The hundred largest employers in the United Kingdom', 96–103.
9. R. J. Irving, *The North Eastern Railway Company, 1870–1914* (Leicester, 1976), 215–16.
10. G. Anderson, *Victorian Clerks* (Manchester, 1976), 10.
11. Ibid. 14.
12. Ibid. 20–6; the reference should perhaps be to the 'first' Baring crisis, since in the second, in 1994, most of the bank's employees succeeded in retaining their bonus payments.
13. F. Capie and G. Wood, 'Money in the economy, 1870–1939', in Floud and McCloskey, *Economic History of Britain*, 225–9.
14. H. Perkin, *The Rise of Professional Society: England since 1800* (London, 1989), 20.
15. L. Urwick and E. F. L. Brech, *The Making of Scientific Management* (London, 1946).
16. Public Record Office RAIL/258/400, 14 Nov. 1900.
17. Briggs, *Victorian Things*, 256–7.
18. A. R. Prest, *Consumers' Expenditure in the United Kingdom, 1900–1919* (Cambridge, 1954), 142.
19. Mitchell, *British Historical Statistics*, 163.

20. Both quotations are taken from Perkin, *Rise of Professional Society*, 77.

21. Ibid. 80, citing Perkin, 'Middle-class education and employment in the 19th century', *Economic History Review*, 14 (1961), 122.

22. Prest, *Consumers' Expenditure*, chap. XXII.

23. S. D. Chapman, *Jesse Boot of Boots the Chemists* (Nottingham, 1974).

24. Private information from R. W. Fogel, based on investigations of the Union Army records for the United States of America.

25. T. McKeown, *The Modern Rise of Population* (London, 1976), 150.

26. Best, *Mid-Victorian Britain*.

27. C. Ehrlich, *The Piano: A History* (Oxford, 1990), 96.

28. Novello and Company, *A Century and a Half in Soho* (London, 1961), 52.

29. Ehrlich, *The Piano*, 96.

30. Quoted ibid. 92.

31. Ibid. 97.

32. Prest, *Consumers' Expenditure*, 132–3.

33. Ehrlich, *The Piano*, 94.

34. W. F. Mandle, 'Games people played: Cricket and football in England and Victoria in the late nineteenth century', *Historical Studies*, 15 (1973).

35. J. K. Walton, *The English Seaside Resort: A Social History 1750–1914* (Leicester, 1983).

36. R. Roberts, 'Leasehold estates and municipal enterprise: landowners, local government and the development of Bournemouth, c.1850–1914', in D. Cannadine (ed.), *Patricians, Power and Politics* (Leicester, 1982).

37. Atkins, 'Sophistication detected', 317–19.

38. J. Birchall, *Co-op: The People's Business* (Manchester, 1994).

39. D. Alexander, *Retailing in England during the Industrial Revolution* (London, 1970), 107–9.

40. J. Morley, *Death, Heaven and the Victorians* (London, 1971), 66–73.

41. Atkins, 'White poison', 207–28.

42. Mathias, *Retailing Revolution*, 45–7.

Chapter 10 (pages 158–170)

1. D. N. McCloskey, *Enterprise and Trade in Victorian Britain: Essays in Historical Economics* (London, 1981).

2. D. Ricardo, *On the Principles of Political Economy and Taxation* (London, 1817), i. 135.

3. Quoted in Briggs, *Victorian Things*, 61.

4. K. Harley, 'Foreign trade: Comparative advantage and performance', in Floud and McCloskey, *Economic History of Britain*, i. 311.

5. J. G. Williamson, 'The impact of the Corn Laws prior to repeal', *Explorations in Economic History*, 27 (1990), 143.

6. Mitchell, *British Historical Statistics*, 229–31.

7. M. Edelstein, 'Foreign investment and accumulation, 1860–1914', in Floud and McCloskey, *Economic History of Britain*, ii. 173–4.

8. M. Edelstein, *Overseas Investment in the Age of High Imperialism. The United Kingdom 1850–1914* (London, 1982) and id., 'Foreign Investment'.

9. Baines, *Migration in a Mature Economy*, 63.

10. M. Edelstein, 'Imperialism: Cost and benefit', in Floud and McCloskey, *Economic History of Britain*, ii. 215–16.

11. Ibid. 214–15.

Chapter 11 (pages 171–185)

1. Samuel Smiles, *Lives of the Engineers* (London, 1861–2) and *Self-Help* (London, 1886).

2. A. T. Peacock and J. Wiseman, *The Growth of Public Expenditure in the United Kingdom* (Princeton, 1961), 37.

3. S. G. Checkland, *British Public Policy, 1776–1939* (Cambridge, 1983), 111, 157, 258, 387.

4. John Stuart Mill, *Principles of Political Economy* (London, 1848), quoted in Peacock and Wiseman, *Growth of Public Expenditure*, 35.

5. Mitchell, *British Historical Statistics*, 104.

6. C. Chester and N. Bowring, *Questions in Parliament* (Oxford, 1962), 87, 316.

7. Checkland, *British Public Policy*, 83–4.

8. Bartrip, 'How green was my valance?', 912–13.

9. A. Offer, *Property and Politics, 1870–1914* (Cambridge, 1981), 105.

10. Ibid. 119.

11. Ibid. 130–1.

12. Ibid. 82.

13. Ibid. 50.

14. Lord Cairns, Lord Chancellor, quoted ibid. 35.

15. Ibid. 84.

16. R. W. Kostal, *Law and English Railway Capitalism, 1825–1875* (Oxford, 1994), 358–66.

17. Checkland, *British Public Policy*, 120.
18. Quoted in Briggs, *Victorian Things*, 378.
19. M. MacKinnon, 'Living standards, 1870–1914', in Floud and McCloskey, *Economic History of Britain*, ii. 285.
20. Ibid. 284.
21. Ibid. 288.

BIBLIOGRAPHY

Much of this book is based on research which is surveyed and reported in two sets of volumes, *The Economic History of Britain since 1700* edited by Roderick Floud and D. N. McCloskey (Cambridge University Press, 3 volumes, 1994) and *The Cambridge Social History of Britain, 1750–1950*, edited by F. M. L. Thompson (Cambridge University Press, 3 volumes, 1990). Each is comprehensive and authoritative and contains an extensive bibliography. A useful visual supplement is the *Atlas of Industrialising Britain, 1780–1914*, edited by J. Langton and R. J. Morris (Methuen, 1986). Supplementary references to particularly useful books and articles on individual topics are given here in the Bibliography and in the Notes.

Statistics of the British economy can be found most conveniently in *British Historical Statistics* edited by B. R. Mitchell (Cambridge University Press, 1988) and in *National Income, Expenditure and Output of the United Kingdom, 1855–1965* by C. H. Feinstein (Cambridge University Press, 1972). The most detailed quantitative treatment of the growth of the economy can be found in *British Economic Growth, 1856–1973* by R. C. O. Matthews, C. H. Feinstein and J. C. Odling-Smee (Clarendon Press, 1982).

Detailed research in British economic and social history is published in *The Economic History Review, The Journal of Economic History, Social History* and *Explorations in Economic History*, which also publish lists and reviews of books. The monthly magazine *History Today* contains many articles on social and economic history for the general reader.

Everyone has a favourite book for someone coming to an historical period for the first time. Mine is *Victorian Things* by Asa Briggs (Penguin, 1988), which combines technology, social and economic history, culture, custom and fashion, art, and design.

Alexander, D., *Retailing in England during the Industrial Revolution* (London, 1970).

Anderson, G., *Victorian Clerks* (Manchester, 1976).

Anderson, M., 'The social implications of demographic change', in Thompson (1990), vol. ii, pp. 1–70.

Atkins, P. J., 'Sophistication detected: Or, the adulteration of the milk supply, 1850–1914', *Social History*, 16 (1991), 317–39.

—— 'White poison: The social consequences of milk consumption in London, 1850–1939', *Social History of Medicine*, 5 (1992), 207–28.

Bagwell, P. S., *The Transport Revolution from 1770* (London, 1974).

Baines, D. E., *Migration in a Mature Economy: Emigration and Internal Migration in England and Wales 1861–1900* (Cambridge, 1985).

—— 'Population, migration and regional development', in Floud and McCloskey (1994), vol. ii.

Barker, M., 'The middle class journey to work in Newcastle upon Tyne, 1850–1913', *Journal of Transport History*, 12 (1991), 107–34.

Bartrip, P. W. J., 'How green was my valance? Environmental arsenic poisoning and the Victorian domestic ideal', *English Historical Review*, 109 (1994), 891–913.

Benson, J., *Coalminers in the Nineteenth Century* (Dublin, 1980).

Best, G., *Mid-Victorian Britain, 1851–70* (London, 1979).

Birchall, J., *Co-op: The People's Business* (Manchester, 1994).

Booth, Charles, *Life and Labour in London* (London, 1892).

Bourke, J., 'Housewifery in working-class England, 1860–1914', *Past and Present*, 143 (1994), 167–97.

Boyd, C. W. (ed.), *Mr Chamberlain's Speeches* (London, 1914).

Boyer, G. R., and Hatton, T. J., 'Did Joseph Arch raise agricultural wages? Rural trade unions and the labour market in late nineteenth-century England', *Economic History Review*, 47 (1994), 310–34.

Briggs, A., *Victorian Things* (London, 1988).

Byatt, I. C. R., *The British Electrical Industry, 1875–1914* (Oxford, 1974).

Cannadine, D. (ed.), *Patricians, Power, and Politics* (Leicester, 1982).

Capie, F., and Wood, G., 'Money in the economy, 1870–1939', in Floud and McCloskey (1994).

Chadwick, Sir Edwin, Supplementary report on the result of a special inquiry into the practice of interment in towns (*Parliamentary Papers* 1843), xii.

Chapman, S. D., *Jesse Boot of Boots the Chemists* (Nottingham, 1974).

Checkland, S. G., *British Public Policy, 1776–1939* (Cambridge, 1983).

Chester, C., and Bowring, N., *Questions in Parliament* (Oxford, 1962).

Chinn, C., *Better Betting with a Decent Feller: Bookmaking, Betting and the British Working Class, 1750–1990* (New York, 1991).

Church, R. A., *The Great Victorian Boom, 1850–1873* (London, 1975).

—— *The History of the British Coal Industry: 1830–1913: Victorian Pre-eminence* (Oxford, 1986).

Cipolla, C. M., *The Industrial Revolution* (London, 1973).

Clapp, B. W., *An Environmental History of Britain* (London, 1994).

Cobbett, W., *Cottage Economy* (London, 1821).

Collins, E. J. T., 'The age of machinery', in Mingay (1981).

Crossick, G., *An Artisan Elite in Victorian Society: Kentish London 1840–1880* (London, 1978).

Cunningham, H., 'Leisure and culture', in Thompson (1990), vol. ii.

Daunton, M. J., *Housing the Workers* (London, 1990).

David, P. A., *Technical Choice, Innovation and Economic Growth: Essays on American and British Experience in the Nineteenth Century* (Cambridge, 1975).

Davidoff, L., 'The family in Britain', in Thompson (1990), vol. ii.

——, and Hall, C., *Family Fortunes: Men and Women of the English Middle Class, 1780–1850* (London, 1992).

Deane, P., and Cole, W. A., *British Economic Growth: 1688–1959* (Cambridge, 1967).

Edelstein, M., *Overseas Investment in the Age of High Imperialism: The United Kingdom 1850–1914* (London, 1982).

—— 'Foreign Investment and Accumulation, 1860–1914', in Floud and McCloskey (1994), vol. ii.

—— 'Imperialism: Cost and benefit', in Floud and McCloskey (1994), vol. ii.

Ehrlich, C., *The Piano: A History* (Oxford, 1990).

Encyclopaedia Britannica (London, 1910).

Falkus, M. E., 'The British Gas industry before 1850', *Economic History Review*, 20 (1967), 494–508.

Feinstein, C. H., *National Income, Expenditure and Output of the United Kingdom, 1855–1965* (Cambridge, 1972).

Floud, R. C., *The British Machine Tool Industry to 1914* (Cambridge, 1976).

——, Wachter, K. W., and Gregory, A., *Height, Health and History: Nutritional Status in the United Kingdom, 1750–1980* (Cambridge, 1992).

——, and McCloskey, D. N. (eds.), *The Economic History of Britain since 1700*, 2nd edn. (3 vols., Cambridge, 1994).

Food and Agriculture Organisation, 'Energy and protein requirements: report of a joint FAO/WHO/UN expert consultation', Technical Report Series 724 (Geneva, 1985).

Frome Wilkinson, J., *The Friendly Society Movement* (1886).

Gatrell, V. A. C., and Hadden, T. B., 'Criminal statistics and their interpretation', in Wrigley (1972).

Girouard, M., *The Victorian Country House* (New Haven, 1979).

Gosden, P. H. J. H., *The Friendly Societies of Britain, 1815–1875* (Manchester, 1961).

Gray, R., 'Medical men, industrial labour and the state in Britain, 1830–1850', *Social History*, 16 (1991), 19–43.

Green, D. R., 'Distance to work in Victorian London: A case study of Henry Poole, Bespoke Tailors', *Business History*, 30 (1988), 179–94.

Grossmith, G., and W., *Diary of a Nobody* (London, 1892).

Guha, S., 'The importance of social intervention in England's mortality decline: The evidence reviewed', *Social History of Medicine*, 7 (1994), 89–114.

Hardy, A., 'Rickets and the rest: Child-care, diet and the infectious children's diseases, 1850–1914', *Social History of Medicine*, 5 (1992), 389–412.

Harley, K., 'Foreign trade: Comparative advantage and performance', in Floud and McCloskey (1994), vol. i.

Hartwell, R. M., 'The service revolution: the growth of services in modern economy 1700–1914', in Cipolla (1973).

Hennock, E. P., *Fit and Proper Persons: Ideal and Reality in Nineteenth Century Urban Government* (London, 1973).

Horrell, S., and Humphries, J., 'Old questions, new data and alternative perspectives: Families' living standards in the industrial revolution', *Journal of Economic History*, 52 (1992), 849–80.

Hunt, E. H., *Regional Wage Variations in Britain, 1850–1914* (Oxford, 1973).

—— *British Labour History* (London, 1981).

Huxley, A., *An Illustrated History of Gardening* (London, 1978).

Irving, R. J., *The North-Eastern Railway Company, 1870–1914* (Leicester, 1976).

Jeremy, D. J., 'The hundred largest employers in the United Kingdom, in manufacturing and non-manufacturing industries, in 1907, 1935 and 1955', *Business History*, 33 (1991), 93–111.

Jevons, H. S., *The British Coal Trade* (London, 1915).

Johnson, P., *Saving and Spending: The Working-Class Economy in Britain, 1870–1939* (Oxford, 1985).

—— 'Small debts and economic distress in England and Wales, 1857–1913', *Economic History Review*, 46 (1993), 65–87.

—— (ed.), *20th Century Britain: Economic, Social and Cultural Change* (Harlow, 1994).

Joyce, P., 'Work', in Thompson (1990).

Kanefsky, J. W., 'Motive power in British industry and the accuracy of the 1870 factory return', *Economic History Review*, 32 (1979), 360–75.

Klingender, F. D. (ed. A. Elton), *Art and the Industrial Revolution* (London, 1968).

Kostal, R. W., *Law and English Railway Capitalism, 1825–1875* (Oxford, 1994).

Langton, J., and Morris, R. J., *Atlas of Industrialising Britain, 1780–1914* (London, 1986).

Lee, C., 'The service industries', in Floud and McCloskey (1994), vol. ii.

Leneman, L., 'Lives and Limbs: Company records as a source for the history of industrial injuries', *Social History of Medicine*, 6 (1993), 405–28.

Levi, L., *Wages and Earnings of the Working Classes* (London, 1867).

McCloskey, D. N., *Enterprise and Trade in Victorian Britain: Essays in Historical Economics* (London, 1981).

McKeown, T., *The Modern Rise of Population* (London, 1976).

McKibbin, R., *The Ideologies of Class: Social Relations in Britain 1880–1950* (Oxford, 1990).

MacKinnon, M., 'Living standards, 1870–1914', in Floud and McCloskey (1994), vol. ii.

Mandle, W. F., 'Games people played: Cricket and football in England and Victoria in the late nineteenth century', *Historical Studies*, 15 (1973).

Masterman, C., *The Condition of England* (London, 1909).

Mathias, P., *Retailing Revolution: A History of Multiple Retailing in the Food Trades Based upon the Allied Suppliers Group of Companies* (London, 1967).

Matthews, R. C. O., Feinstein, C. H., and Odling-Smee, J. C., *British Economic Growth 1856–1973* (Oxford, 1982).

Mill, J. S., 'The spirit of the age' (1831), in G. L. Williams (ed.), *Mill on Politics and Society* (Hassocks, 1976), 171.

—— *Principles of Political Economy* (London, 1848).

Millward, R., and Sheard, S., 'Government expenditure on social overheads and the infrastructure in England and Wales, 1870–1914', *University of Manchester Working Papers in Economic and Social History*, 23 (1993).

Mingay, G. E., *The Victorian Countryside* (London, 1981).

Mitchell, B. R., *British Historical Statistics* (Cambridge, 1988).

More, C., *Skill and the English Working Class, 1870–1914* (London, 1980).

Morley, J., *Death, Heaven and the Victorians* (London, 1971).

Newman, G., *Bacteriology and the Public Health* (London, 1904).

Novello and Company, *A Century and a Half in Soho* (London, 1961).

Oddy, D. J., 'Food, drink and nutrition', in Thompson (1990).

Offer, A., *Property and Politics, 1870–1914* (Cambridge, 1981).

O'Grada, C., 'British agriculture 1860–1914', in Floud and McCloskey (1994), vol. ii.

Olsen, D. J., *The Growth of Victorian London* (Harmondsworth, 1979).

Overton, M., 'Agriculture', in Langton and Morris (1986).

Parliamentary Papers, *Report of His Majesty's Commissioners for Inquiring into the Administration and Practical Operation of the Poor Laws* (PP, 1834), xxxvi.

Parliamentary Papers, *Report on a General Scheme for Extra Mural Sepulture* (PP, 1850), xxi.

Peacock, A. T., and Wiseman, J., *The Growth of Public Expenditure in the United Kingdom* (Princeton, 1961).

Perkin, H., 'Middle-class education and employment in the 19th century', *Economic History Review*, 14 (1961), 122.

—— *The Rise of Professional Society: England since 1880* (London, 1989).

Powell, C. G., *An Economic History of the British Building Industry, 1815–1979* (London, 1980).

Preece, W. H., 'Recent progress in telephony', *Journal of the Society of Arts*, 30 (1882), 965–9.

Prest, A. R., *Consumers' Expenditure in the United Kingdom, 1900–1919* (Cambridge, 1954).

Redford, A., *Manchester Merchants and Foreign Trade* (Manchester, 1956), vol. ii.

Ricardo, D., *On the Principles of Political Economy and Taxation* (London, 1817).

Richardson, C. J., *Rus in Urbe: Or Flowers that Thrive in London Gardens or Smoky Towns* (London, 1886).

Riley, J. C., *Sickness, Recovery and Death: A history and forecast of ill-health* (London, 1989).

Roberts, E., *A Woman's Place: An Oral History of Working-class Women, 1890–1940* (Oxford, 1984).

Roberts, R., 'Leasehold estates and municipal enterprise: landowners, local government and the development of Bournemouth, c.1850–1914', in Cannadine (ed.) (1982).

Robson, B. T., *Urban Growth: An Approach* (London, 1973).

Rosenberg, N. (ed.), *The American System of Manufactures* (Edinburgh, 1969).

Rowe, D. J., 'The North East', in Thompson (1990), vol. i.

Rowntree, B. Seebohm, *Poverty: A Study of Town Life* (London, 1901).

Royal Commission, *The Employment of Women and Children in Agriculture* (PP, 1843), xii, 1–377.

Royal Commission, *The Pollution of Rivers* (1867).

Select Committee, *Injury from Noxious Vapours* (PP, 1862), xiv. 1.

Smelser, N. J., *Social Change in the Industrial Revolution: An application of theory to the Lancashire cotton industry, 1770–1840* (London, 1959).

Smiles, S., *Lives of the Engineers* (London, 1861–2).

—— *Self-Help* (London, 1886).

Smith, A., *The Wealth of Nations* (1776).

Smith, D., 'Sir William Bazalgette', *Transactions of the Newcomen Society*, 58 (1986–7).

Smith, S., Article in *The Edinburgh Review*, 19 Jan. 1820.

Snell, K. D. M., 'Agricultural seasonal unemployment: the standard of living and women's work in the south and east, 1690–1860', *Economic History Review*, 34 (1981), 407–37.

Southall, H., and Garrett, E., 'Morbidity and mortality among early nineteenth century engineering workers', *Social History of Medicine*, 4 (1991), 231–53.

Stedman-Jones, G., *Outcast London* (Oxford, 1971).

Supple, B. S., *The Royal Exchange Assurance: A History of British Insurance 1720–1970* (Cambridge, 1970).

Sutherland, G., 'Education', in Thompson (1990), vol. iii.

Szreter, S., 'The importance of social intervention in Britain's mortality decline c.1850–1914: A reinterpretation of the role of public health', *Social History of Medicine*, 1 (1988), 1–38.

Thane, P., 'Government and society in England and Wales, 1750–1914', in Thompson (1990).

Thompson, F. M. L., *The Cambridge Social History of Britain, 1750–1950* (3 vols., Cambridge, 1990).

Treble, J. H., *Urban Poverty in Britain, 1830–1914* (London, 1979).

Tressell, R., *The Ragged Trousered Philanthropists* (London, 1914).

Urwick, L., and Brech, E. F. L., *The Making of Scientific Management* (London, 1946).

Veblen, T., *The Theory of the Leisure Class* (London, 1925).

von Tunzelmann, G. N., *Steam Power and British Industrialization to 1860* (Oxford, 1978).

Walton, J. K., *The English Seaside Resort: A social history 1750–1914* (Leicester, 1983).

—— *Fish and Chips and the British Working Class, 1870–1940* (Leicester, 1992).

Warren, K., *Armstrongs of Elswick: Growth in Engineering and Armaments to the merger with Vickers* (London, 1989).

Weir, R. B., 'Brewing and distilling', in Langton and Morris (1986).

Wiener, M., *English Culture and the Decline of the Industrial Spirit* (Cambridge, 1981).

Williams, E. E., *Made in Germany* (London, 1896).

Williamson, J. G., 'The structure of pay in Britain, 1710–1911', *Research in Economic History*, 7 (1982).

—— 'The impact of the Corn Laws prior to repeal', *Explorations in Economic History*, 27 (1990), 123–56.

Wohl, A. S., *Endangered Lives: Public Health in Victorian Britain* (London, 1983).

Wrigley, E. A., *Nineteenth Century Society: Essays in the Use of Quantitative Methods for the Study of Social Data* (Cambridge, 1972).

INDEX

OXFORD

MORE OXFORD PAPERBACKS

This book is just one of nearly 1000 Oxford Paperbacks currently in print. If you would like details of other Oxford Paperbacks, including titles in the World's Classics, Oxford Reference, Oxford Books, OPUS, Past Masters, Oxford Authors, and Oxford Shakespeare series, please write to:

UK and Europe: Oxford Paperbacks Publicity Manager, Arts and Reference Publicity Department, Oxford University Press, Walton Street, Oxford OX2 6DP.

Customers in UK and Europe will find Oxford Paperbacks available in all good bookshops. But in case of difficulty please send orders to the Cash-with-Order Department, Oxford University Press Distribution Services, Saxon Way West, Corby, Northants NN18 9ES. Tel: 01536 741519; Fax: 01536 746337. Please send a cheque for the total cost of the books, plus £1.75 postage and packing for orders under £20; £2.75 for orders over £20. Customers outside the UK should add 10% of the cost of the books for postage and packing.

USA: Oxford Paperbacks Marketing Manager, Oxford University Press, Inc., 200 Madison Avenue, New York, N.Y. 10016.

Canada: Trade Department, Oxford University Press, 70 Wynford Drive, Don Mills, Ontario M3C 1J9.

Australia: Trade Marketing Manager, Oxford University Press, G.P.O. Box 2784Y, Melbourne 3001, Victoria.

South Africa: Oxford University Press, P.O. Box 1141, Cape Town 8000.

LAW FROM OXFORD PAPERBACKS

INTRODUCTION TO ENGLISH LAW
Tenth Edition

William Geldart

Edited by D. C. M. Yardley

'Geldart' has over the years established itself as a standard account of English law, expounding the body of modern law as set in its historical context. Regularly updated since its first publication, it remains indispensable to student and layman alike as a concise, reliable guide.

Since publication of the ninth edition in 1984 there have been important court decisions and a great deal of relevant new legislation. D. C. M. Yardley, Chairman of the Commission for Local Administration in England, has taken account of all these developments and the result has been a considerable rewriting of several parts of the book. These include the sections dealing with the contractual liability of minors, the abolition of the concept of illegitimacy, the liability of a trade union in tort for inducing a person to break his/her contract of employment, the new public order offences, and the intent necessary for a conviction of murder.

HISTORY IN OXFORD PAPERBACKS
TUDOR ENGLAND
John Guy

Tudor England is a compelling account of political and religious developments from the advent of the Tudors in the 1460s to the death of Elizabeth I in 1603.

Following Henry VII's capture of the Crown at Bosworth in 1485, Tudor England witnessed far-reaching changes in government and the Reformation of the Church under Henry VIII, Edward VI, Mary, and Elizabeth; that story is enriched here with character studies of the monarchs and politicians that bring to life their personalities as well as their policies.

Authoritative, clearly argued, and crisply written, this comprehensive book will be indispensable to anyone interested in the Tudor Age.

'lucid, scholarly, remarkably accomplished . . . an excellent overview' *Sunday Times*

'the first comprehensive history of Tudor England for more than thirty years' Patrick Collinson, *Observer*

HISTORY IN OXFORD PAPERBACKS

THE STRUGGLE FOR
THE MASTERY OF EUROPE 1848–1918

A. J. P. Taylor

The fall of Metternich in the revolutions of 1848 heralded an era of unprecedented nationalism in Europe, culminating in the collapse of the Hapsburg, Romanov, and Hohenzollern dynasties at the end of the First World War. In the intervening seventy years the boundaries of Europe changed dramatically from those established at Vienna in 1815. Cavour championed the cause of *Risorgimento* in Italy; Bismarck's three wars brought about the unification of Germany; Serbia and Bulgaria gained their independence courtesy of the decline of Turkey—'the sick man of Europe'; while the great powers scrambled for places in the sun in Africa. However, with America's entry into the war and President Wilson's adherence to idealistic internationalist principles, Europe ceased to be the centre of the world, although its problems, still primarily revolving around nationalist aspirations, were to smash the Treaty of Versailles and plunge the world into war once more.

A. J. P. Taylor has drawn the material for his account of this turbulent period from the many volumes of diplomatic documents which have been published in the five major European languages. By using vivid language and forceful characterization, he has produced a book that is as much a work of literature as a contribution to scientific history.

'One of the glories of twentieth-century writing.'
Observer

PAST MASTERS

A wide range of unique, short, clear introductions to the lives and work of the world's most influential thinkers. Written by experts, they cover the history of ideas from Aristotle to Wittgenstein. Readers need no previous knowledge of the subject, so they are ideal for students and general readers alike.

Each book takes as its main focus the thought and work of its subject. There is a short section on the life and a final chapter on the legacy and influence of the thinker. A section of further reading helps in further research.

The series continues to grow, and future Past Masters will include **Owen Gingerich** on *Copernicus*, **R G Frey** on *Joseph Butler*, **Bhiku Parekh** on *Gandhi*, **Christopher Taylor** on *Socrates*, **Michael Inwood** on *Heidegger*, and **Peter Ghosh** on *Weber*.

PAST MASTERS

General Editor: Keith Thomas

HOBBES

Richard Tuck

Thomas Hobbes (1588–1679) was the first great English political philosopher, and his book *Leviathan* was one of the first truly modern works of philosophy. He has long had the reputation of being a pessimistic atheist, who saw human nature as inevitably evil, and who proposed a totalitarian state to subdue human failings. In this new study, Richard Tuck shows that while Hobbes may indeed have been an atheist, he was far from pessimistic about human nature, nor did he advocate totalitarianism. By locating him against the context of his age, Dr Tuck reveals Hobbes to have been passionately concerned with the refutation of scepticism in both science and ethics, and to have developed a theory of knowledge which rivalled that of Descartes in its importance for the formation of modern philosophy.

MASTERS

KEYNES

Robert Skidelsky

John Maynard Keynes is a central thinker of the twentieth century. This is the only available short introduction to his life and work.

Keynes's doctrines continue to inspire strong feelings in admirers and detractors alike. This short, engaging study of his life and thought explores the many positive and negative stereotypes and also examines the quality of Keynes's mind, his cultural and social milieu, his ethical and practical philosophy, and his monetary thought. Recent scholarship has significantly altered the treatment and assessment of Keynes's contribution to twentieth-century economic thinking, and the current state of the debate initiated by the Keynesian revolution is discussed in a final chapter on its legacy.

PAST
MASTERS

RUSSELL

A. C. *Grayling*

Bertrand Russell (1872–1970) is one of the most famous and important philosophers of the twentieth century. In this account of his life and work A. C. Grayling introduces both his technical contributions to logic and philosophy, and his wide-ranging views on education, politics, war, and sexual morality. Russell is credited with being one of the prime movers of Analytic Philosophy, and with having played a part in the revolution in social attitudes witnessed throughout the twentieth-century world. This introduction gives a clear survey of Russell's achievements across their whole range.

THE CONCISE OXFORD DICTIONARY
OF POLITICS

Edited by Iain McLean

Written by an expert team of political scientists from Warwick University, this is the most authoritative and up-to-date dictionary of politics available.

* Over 1,500 entries provide truly international coverage of major political institutions, thinkers and concepts

* From Western to Chinese and Muslim political thought

* Covers new and thriving branches of the subject, including international political economy, voting theory, and feminism

* Appendix of political leaders

* Clear, no-nonsense definitions of terms such as veto and subsidiarity

OXFORD

FOUR ESSAYS ON LIBERTY

Isaiah Berlin

'*those who value liberty for its own sake believe that to be free to choose, and not to be chosen for, is an inalienable ingredient in what makes human beings human*'
Introduction to *Four Essays On Liberty*

Political Ideas in the Twentieth Century
Historical Inevitability
Two Concepts of Liberty
John Stuart Mill and the Ends of Life

These four essays deal with the various aspects of individual liberty, including the distinction between positive and negative liberty and the necessity of rejecting determinism if we wish to keep hold of the notions of human responsibility and freedom.

'practically every paragraph introduces us to half a dozen new ideas and as many thinkers—the landscape flashes past, peopled with familiar and unfamiliar people, all arguing incessantly'
New Society

WORLD'S ✿ CLASSICS

PRINCIPLES OF HUMAN KNOWLEDGE AND THREE DIALOGUES

GEORGE BERKELEY

Edited by Howard Robinson

Berkeley's idealism started a revolution in philosophy. As one of the great empiricist thinkers he not only influenced British philosophers from Hume to Russell and the logical positivists in the twentieth century, he also set the scene for the continental idealism of Hegel and even the philosophy of Marx.

There has never been such a radical critique of common sense and perception as that given in Berkeley's *Principles of Human Knowledge* (1710). His views were met with disfavour, and his response to his critics was the *Three Dialogues* between Hylas and Philonous.

This edition of Berkeley's two key works has an introduction which examines and in part defends his arguments for idealism, as well as offering a detailed analytical contents list, extensive philosophical notes and an index.

PHILOSOPHY IN OXFORD PAPERBACKS
THE GREAT PHILOSOPHERS
Bryan Magee

Beginning with the death of Socrates in 399, and following the story through the centuries to recent figures such as Bertrand Russell and Wittgenstein, Bryan Magee and fifteen contemporary writers and philosophers provide an accessible and exciting introduction to Western philosophy and its greatest thinkers.

Bryan Magee in conversation with:

A. J. Ayer	John Passmore
Michael Ayers	Anthony Quinton
Miles Burnyeat	John Searle
Frederick Copleston	Peter Singer
Hubert Dreyfus	J. P. Stern
Anthony Kenny	Geoffrey Warnock
Sidney Morgenbesser	Bernard Williams
Martha Nussbaum	

'Magee is to be congratulated . . . anyone who sees the programmes or reads the book will be left in no danger of believing philosophical thinking is unpractical and uninteresting.' Ronald Hayman, *Times Educational Supplement*

'one of the liveliest, fast-paced introductions to philosophy, ancient and modern that one could wish for' *Universe*